A Starter on Support-Bargaining and Money-Bargaining in Twenty-Eight Digestible Bites

Patrick Spread

A Starter on Support-Bargaining and Money-Bargaining in Twenty-Eight Digestible Bites

palgrave
macmillan

Patrick Spread
Witney, Oxfordshire, UK

ISBN 978-3-030-05230-0   ISBN 978-3-030-05231-7 (eBook)
https://doi.org/10.1007/978-3-030-05231-7

Library of Congress Control Number: 2018962919

Cover illustration: Pattern adapted from an Indian cotton print produced in the 19th century

This Palgrave Pivot imprint is published by the registered company Springer Nature Switzerland AG
The registered company address is: Gewerbestrasse 11, 6330 Cham, Switzerland

Contents

CHAPTER 1

Appetiser

Abstract The Appetiser suggests that the neoclassical economic model responds to a conjecture regarding the relationship between private and public interest rather than a question about the working of economic exchange. The *Starter* explains economic exchange. To explain economic exchange, it is first necessary to explain the process of 'support-bargaining' and the creation of money. With that, it is possible to explain how money is used in 'money-bargaining', the process of economic exchange. The Appetiser also identifies 'communal interests' as outcomes of support-bargaining. Money-bargaining accommodates communal interests as well as the individual interests that are the basic concern of neoclassical theory.

Keywords Support-bargaining · Money creation · Money-bargaining · Neoclassical theory · Economic exchange · Communal interest

Psychologists have noted that when asked a question, people often answer a different question which they find easier to respond to. Neoclassical economic theory, or 'mainstream' economic theory, seems a good illustration of the phenomenon. Instead of answering the question, 'How does economic exchange work?' neoclassical economists have answered a different question: 'What does a system look like in which

P. Spread, *A Starter on Support-Bargaining and Money-Bargaining in Twenty-Eight Digestible Bites*,
https://doi.org/10.1007/978-3-030-05231-7_1

the pursuit of private interest leads to the fulfilment of public interest?' The answer to the different question is the neoclassical economic model.

The first question is the subject of this 'Starter'. The answer requires first an answer to the broader question: 'How does social and political society work?' 'Democracy' provides a fine set of principles but does not explain how 'democracies' actually function. It is suggested that they function through 'support-bargaining'. People need support from those around them as a matter of personal security, and will change their opinions and behaviour to get it. Individuals instinctively bargain for support with each other and in the process form groups committed to certain interests, actions, ideas, opinions and theories. The mutual support of members promotes confidence in a group regarding the rightness of its commitments, however odd they may appear to non-members. 'Support' functions as a bargaining counter in a bargaining process through which individual interests and group or social interests become adjusted to each other.

It is then possible to answer the first question. Amongst the varied outcomes of the support-bargaining process is 'money'. 'Money' gains support in a community because it is useful in a bargaining process with a similar dynamic to that of support-bargaining. 'Money' is a precise and divisible bargaining counter particularly useful in transactions involving items with similar qualities. 'Support' is a matter of psychology, lacking the characteristics desirable in a bargaining counter for use in economic transactions. So long as a form of money has the support of the community in which it is used, it will function as a bargaining counter in a process of 'money-bargaining'. So, the answer to the first question is that economic exchange is a money-bargaining system.

Mainstream economic theory recognises the 'public interest' as the 'optimal allocation of resources' arising from the pursuit of private interest through economic transactions. The outcome is optimal in the sense that no redistribution of resources can make anyone better off without making others worse off. Few would recognise this as being the public interest in any but a technical sense. The idea of support-bargaining makes apparent that a great variety of group or communal interests can be identified through support-bargaining. It is then necessary to realise through money-bargaining not just the individual interests that are the concern of neoclassical theory, but also communal interests. To accommodate communal interests, it has been found possible to make levies on private money-bargaining, without disabling private money-bargaining systems, to provide revenues for government budgets. Money can then be disbursed for the accommodation of communal interests. Support-bargaining agencies, including political parties and governments, are accorded responsibility for communal interests. Governments are able to realise communal interests through budgetary expenditures. They become part of money-bargaining systems. Money-bargaining systems are concerned with both individual and communal interests.

* * * *

This *Starter* provides an account of support-bargaining, the formation of theories through support-bargaining, the origins of money-bargaining in support-bargaining, the dynamic of money-bargaining and the interrelation of money-bargaining and support-bargaining. It evaluates the role of information in human affairs. It explains also how it is that mainstream theory has emerged as the mainstream when it so manifestly fails to provide a faithful account of the dynamic of economic exchange. There is little that is novel, but the *Starter* is not simply a summary of previous work. It is a new expression of the theory of support-bargaining and money-bargaining. The compact format makes apparent the relationship of the different components to each other. It provides direct answers to the questions thrown up by the many who challenge the mainstream model. It provides a new account of economic exchange, but one that will be instantly recognised as consistent with everyday experience.

'The Main Course', at the end of the book, provides summaries of the contents of the seven books already published on support-bargaining and money-bargaining.

'Notes from the Kitchen' at the end of each chapter identify the main coverage of the issues of each bite in earlier books, with an indication also of the main sources used. A full account of the sources used is provided in the earlier books.

Notes from the Kitchen

Sources

The Introduction to *Economics for an Information Age* (EIA) considers responses to questions. Chapter 9 of Kahneman (2012) is 'Answering an Easier Question'.

References

Kahneman, Daniel, 2012, *Thinking, Fast and Slow*, Penguin.

Spread, Patrick, 2019, *Economics for an Information Age: Money-Bargaining, Support-Bargaining and the Information Interface (EIA)*, Routledge.

CHAPTER 2

Support and Support-Bargaining

Abstract Support-bargaining arises from the need of all individuals for the support of those around them. It leads to the formation of groups and the identification of group interests. High cohesion is necessary to the effectiveness of groups, most readily achieved when a group is under external threat. Individuals and groups identify their interests by reference to their situation. Humans use their sense of symmetry to determine what will 'fit' their situation. Situation-related interest causes societies to evolve from situation to situation. In a threatening situation, individuals will recognise that their individual interest is inseparable from that of the group. This can give rise to rigid groups, with the extreme cohesion necessary to violent action. Groups organise, with hierarchies and budgets, to increase their effectiveness.

Keywords Support-bargaining · Group interest · External threat · Social evolution · Organisations · Symmetry

BITE 1: THE IMPORTANCE OF SUPPORT

One enduring feature of human behaviour is that we seek reassurance. Children run to a parent at the first sign of trouble. Adults complain to their friends in the expectation of reassurance that they are put upon, or the trouble is not so bad. Humans have an innate sense of insecurity and the necessary remedy for that insecurity is the support of others.

P. Spread, *A Starter on Support-Bargaining and Money-Bargaining in Twenty-Eight Digestible Bites*,
https://doi.org/10.1007/978-3-030-05231-7_2

It is, perhaps, at the most basic level, a concern for self-preservation in a threatening world. Security comes only with the assurance from others that they are on our side, are with us. Social media like Facebook and Twitter help people to obtain the reassurance they need.

Such support does not come free. It has to be earned. At the very least, we have to perform the same offices of reassurance for our friends. If we do not support them, they will not support us. But support derives not just from reassurance against specific troubles, but the reassurance that arises from shared opinions and actions that benefit the group. We adjust our opinions and behaviour to gain the approval of those around us, in the expectation of ongoing support from the group.

Behaviour that elicits support includes what is called 'altruistic' behaviour. Altruistic behaviour implies that individuals disregard their own interests to serve the interests of their community. It is difficult to reconcile with the self-seeking dynamic of human evolution by natural selection. But if 'support' is a psychological necessity, individuals gain an essential return from the performance of altruistic acts.

The importance of this sort of support can be seen in the language we use to communicate. By choice of words, we can signal to those we are speaking to the responses we expect from them. If we say, 'good morning' to someone, we elicit a little support, for it is customary to regard all mornings as 'good'. If we refer to someone as 'slim', we expect the person we are addressing to respond in favourable terms about the person referred to. But a reference to someone as 'skinny' is a prompt for disapproval of the person in question. Language has inbuilt facility for directing support and opposition in desired directions and reducing the risk of people failing to provide the desired support.

'Support-bargaining' is conceived as the underlying process by which individual insecurity is allayed by 'negotiations' with associates. It gives rise to the formation of groups. People support each other when they find their views and opinions in accord, meaning also accord over corresponding actions and behaviour. People find security in a group of like-minded persons. The 'negotiations' are largely instinctive and unnoticed. Individual opinions may change, but that may be no more than a subtle inflection of opinion through adoption of the vocabulary used by the group. We become 'instituted' in society, into various social groups and sub-groups. If individuals are so fixed in their opinions and behaviour that they cannot make the necessary adjustments to the group with which they are immediately in contact, they are likely to move on in search of associates who are more accommodating. In Britain, many sports are or have been associated with social groups. Foxhunting up to about the middle of the twentieth century in Britain was notoriously the preserve of people of superior status. Stories about hunts-people suggest they were adept at letting aspiring members know whether they measured up. Joining a golf club can, for some people, mark their elevation to a higher social status. Tennis is seen as a 'middle class' sport. The annual tennis tournament at the All England Tennis and Croquet Club in Wimbledon is a showcase of middle class style. Cycling clubs kept to the left. Herne Hill, the South London velodrome, was decidedly proletarian. These distinctions and associations are replicated in many other walks of life. Support-bargaining involves endless negotiation and renegotiation as people settle into the human surroundings in which they feel comfortable.

The process is of profound significance. It was probably essential to the survival of the species. Charles Darwin does not concern himself with humans in *The Origin of Species*. Readers are left to deduce for themselves the implications for humans of natural selection amongst animals and plants. But in *The Descent of Man*, Darwin turned his attention to the human species. He recognised that group formation was necessary to survival. Without the cooperation implicit in group formation, a species would not be an effective fighting force, and consequently its survival would be in doubt. Darwin was unable to identify, even to his own satisfaction, how groups were formed. His failure can be traced to his emphasis on 'aggression' as the key factor in the survival of the human species, which involved a corresponding eclipse of the instinct for 'self-preservation'. In Darwin's account, 'self-preservation' is an ignoble instinct. It stops a man from fulfilling the obligations that society imposes upon him. A man may refrain from jumping into a tumultuous river to save a stranger, as is his obligation to the society that nurtured him, if he is imbued with the ignoble instinct of self-preservation. Darwin understood 'self-preservation' in accordance with the values of a militaristic society which cultivated bravery and individual self-sacrifice. But according to popular understanding, 'a man's first instinct is self-preservation'. Our psychological reflexes include alerts to threats to our security that take priority over other perceptions. 'Self-preservation' may be deemed socially ignoble, because it is potentially damaging to the defence of the society, but it is the essential impulse behind the sense of insecurity that causes humans to seek support, and hence to form groups. The characteristic that seems at first sight so potentially damaging turns out to be the characteristic that is most important to the survival of a society. Thomas Malthus, the economist from whom Darwin derived much of his emphasis on aggression, and the British military culture, put Darwin off the scent. The vulnerability of humans makes them seek support.

The significance of support is perhaps immediately apparent to everyone in consideration of the pleasure gained from simple expressions of support, approval or congratulation, and from the pain experienced on receipt of disapproval and censure. There is neuroscientific evidence for the pain that arises from the withdrawal of support. Neuroscientists have found that expressions implying social exclusion, which can be construed as expressions implying withdrawal of support, trigger activity in the same centres of the brain as give rise to sensations of physical pain. The researchers suggest that this mechanism of social bonding was originally important for the survival of the human species and subsequently became important as the basis of human social cooperation. Cultural evolution rode on the back of the mental characteristics that were crucial to our survival as a species. Such findings confirm the universal attraction of support that makes possible its use as a bargaining counter. The neuroscientific evidence also makes the link between the psychology of 'support' and the biology of the brain, and hence to the biological variations necessary to survival that were the chief concern of Darwin.

Support-bargaining is a central part of relationships between humans, but it is not the entirety of such relationships. Our relationships are more complex than can be pinned down to one single trait. We love some and hate others; we have affection for some and aversion or animosities towards others; we have sympathies and empathies. These qualities are not necessarily support-seeking or support-denying, though they may affect the way support-bargaining is conducted. They are not normally regarded as 'negotiable' in the way support is here conceived as 'negotiated'. They seem to derive from psychological characteristics other than those that drive us to seek support. They affect the way humans come together and behave towards each other.

But while such traits are not necessarily support-seeking, there may still be in them an element of concern for the assembly of support from associates—the element relating to reassurance and security. Loving relationships are more than reassurance, but reassurance is woven into such relationships. The vocabulary of love prominently includes expressions of care and protection. There is concern for support, even though eclipsed by the presence of other emotions. This 'support' is manifest in the contracts made in virtually all societies between lovers who want to commit to one another for life. Support-bargaining distils from the complexity of human relations a certain strand in relationships that seems critical to the explanation of outcomes.

Bite 2: Support-Bargaining: Individual and Group

The 'bargaining' in support-bargaining concerns the extent to which the interests of an individual will be adopted as group interest, or the extent to which the interests of the group will predominate over individual interest. Individuals need group support. Groups need individual members. Each will be inclined to concede as little as possible to the other. Whatever concessions are made will be made in anticipation of some compensating return. Individuals will find themselves obliged to concede most when they have least to offer a group. Groups will concede most to those individuals they identify as having qualities potentially advantageous to the advance of group interests. All individuals will seek to advance their individual interest, but at the same time, all will have a sense of group identity, and consequently an interest in ensuring that their group is not undermined by concessions to individuals whose inclinations they see as inimical to their group.

Strengthening of a group will depend on assimilation of individuals who can effectively advance group interests. Groups involved with violence will welcome most readily individuals who show capacity for violence, whether physical strength or capacity for military command. Groups concerned with the promotion of supernatural belief will accommodate most easily individuals who can inspire people to belief by their rhetoric or by their pious example. Christians who recognised the failings of the Roman Catholic Church welcomed Martin Luther as the leader of a protestant church. Intellectual groups will welcome those whose mental capacities suggest they will advance whatever branch of learning is the focus of the group. Sportspeople will welcome prowess that promises to take their team to new heights. Political parties are inclined to accept more of the policy preferences of those they see as possessing the rhetorical skills and personal traits of political leaders than of those who have limited skills in the propagation of political ideas. Groups review and revise their group commitments in response to the need to incorporate those individuals who promise best to advance the interests of the group.

The terms on which individuals are assimilated into groups depend also on the range of options open to any individual. If there are numerous sources of support, numerous associations open to an individual, then he or she will be less inclined to make concessions of opinion and behaviour to any one set of associates. The individual will look around for a group whose opinions and conduct require the least compromise. Individuals look for groups where they will 'fit in'; or where their talents will be best rewarded.

Modern societies offer many options for individuals. Most people find associates who accept their inclinations and opinions with adjustments that are easily made. But in earlier societies, such fragmentation was regarded as potentially threatening to the society as a whole. In violent times, fragmented groups are weak groups, and liable to elimination by others. Unity is essential to security and defence. Hence, societies have historically been unwilling to tolerate significant deviation from the opinions and behaviour defined as proper by the group. Individuals have been obliged to concede their inclinations and opinions to the group, often under threat of severe reprisals.

From the earliest times, human groups would have recognised that cohesion, sticking together, gave them a sense of security, essential as it was to their effectiveness in any violence necessary to their survival. They would have recognised also that harmony of understanding was a necessary part of group cohesion. Shared belief in some supernatural phenomenon could augment ties of support deriving simply from the sense of physical insecurity. The placation of deities to attract their support for the group enhanced its cohesion and raised its chances of survival. It frequently became a condition of continued group membership that the appropriate conduct towards deities was observed. While support-bargaining in circumstances of violence leads to the formation of tight and intolerant groups, the diminution of physical threats has led to a great proliferation of groups with different group ideas and purposes.

The importance of group cohesion to effective physical violence, and the recognition that belief in supernatural phenomena could attract such volumes and intensity of support as to be highly effective in achieving group cohesion, meant that rulers of societies were obliged to take into account the religious beliefs of their followers. Whether from personal conviction, or as a matter of political strategy, they were obliged themselves to follow the teachings of the religious leaders of their societies. In most European nations and states, government was carried on through an alliance of monarch and church, 'throne and altar'. The churches constituted in earlier times much of the intellectual life of nations, so that the alliance was characterised also as that of 'sword and pen'. Today, theories and ideologies play much of the part formerly played by religious ideas. They assemble support for the individualist or group factions in Western societies.

Religious faith in all societies has constituted one of the central components of what is referred to as 'culture'. Culture is created through support-bargaining. It comprises all the beliefs, customs, festivals, buildings, works of art, food, attitudes, modes of working, educational provision, theories, provisions for marriage and so on by which communities live almost without consciousness of the artificiality of their culture as something created by themselves and their forebears from instinct and the circumstances of their lives. Cultures are created and evolve through support-bargaining. Children are assimilated into their cultural group—an important element of all cultures is the education and social training they provide for their children. Different circumstances give rise to different interests, so that support moves from one interest to another. New groups emerge and the culture evolves. Some elements of culture endure for centuries but others are ephemeral.

People derive the support necessary to their security from those who are members of their cultural group. People feel at ease with people who share their culture. The social group characteristics of the various sports referred to in Bite 1 are a consequence of the soothing effects of cultural affinity. Immigrant and expatriate groups tend to settle together, to enjoy the benefits of cultural affinities away from home. People of different cultures tend to be less at ease with each other, being aware of the risks of saying the wrong thing, or breaching some cultural rule of behaviour, or being unable to share the cultural prejudices that are acceptable amongst people of their own culture. Groups with shared culture, including whole societies, create as part of their cultural formulations, stereotypes of other cultures, generally unflattering, that help to cement their own cohesion.

Cultural affiliations are displayed in language, accents, body-language, clothing and personal grooming, such as hair styles, growth of beards and use of cosmetics. In Britain, at least certain physical facial characteristics are associated with class affiliations. Racial characteristics—the shape of eyes, the colour of skin—suggest cultural differences. People may shy away from those with different racial characteristics from themselves, for fear of being unable to cope with a different culture, or from fear of rejection.

The support-bargaining between individuals and groups leads to the formation of group opinions, ideas, behaviour, commitments and objectives, or more generally, the formation of a sense of group or communal interest. In a support-bargaining system, there is a sense of communal interest as well as of individual interest. This has significant implications for the understanding of economic systems, or money-bargaining. Mainstream economic theory is built on the assumption of individual interest alone, while the communal interest is given theoretical expression in 'socialist' theory. In the idea of a money-bargaining system, being adjunct to a support-bargaining system (Bite 14), there is necessity for the accommodation of the communal interest, as well as individual interest. The accommodation of communal interest is described in Bite 20.

Bite 3: Situation-Related Interest, Social Evolution and the Sense of Symmetry

Our existing personal and domestic arrangements form the basis for determining what will improve them. If food is going bad, we need a fridge to keep it fresh. Then if we go shopping, we first check what is in the fridge and buy what is necessary to restore stocks to the best level. If we are buying a house, we buy one large enough to accommodate the family, and we buy in a location that will permit access to our employment. Choice and selection are made by reference to situation. By some oversight, social theory, including economic theory, neglects this very fundamental trait.

Groups form on the basis of shared interests, and shared interests emerge from shared situations. People sharing interests coalesce into the groups of communal interest referred to in Bite 2. People in similar situations will find it easier to agree their interests and support one another to realise them. Villagers threatened with a new housing estate nearby may get together to oppose the new development. People with children may get together to ensure that a village school is functioning effectively. Changes of the widest significance come about because of shared situations. Workers in nineteenth-century Europe shared the hardships of employment in factories and came together in trade unions. In Britain, the labour movement and the Labour Party grew out of shared interests in improvement of the appalling living conditions of working men and women in the new industrial towns. The people of Britain came together to protect their territory and way of life against Nazi Germany. In a situation of external threat, individuals recognise that their own interests are inextricably tied in with the interests of the group, and the society will become cohesive to sustain its defence. From the trivial to the existential, our circumstances dictate our interests.

An important implication of this is that societies evolve from situation to situation. Interests are identified by reference to a certain situation, and action is taken to realise those interests. The situation is thereby altered, and will generate a further set of interests. Societies roll on from one situation to another. Those organisations seeking to assemble support will try to ensure that people understand 'situation' in a way that generates support for their interests and the programmes they propose, so that their society evolves to their advantage. The process can be seen in the formation of the labour movement and Labour Party in Britain. Living conditions in the new industrial towns required remedies that brought about new organisations and new political arrangements, which in their turn produced further radical change. Societies evolve through support-bargaining and the movement of support to advance communal interests, advancing some interests in preference to others. Political, cultural and economic evolution all have the same dynamic.

It is a different dynamic to that of evolution by natural selection. Natural selection involves random variation, whereas the concept of social evolution proposed here is an outcome of human volition, applied both instinctively and with forethought. We pursue our interests largely without thinking too much about them. We instinctively seek support and give support to people and actions that seem likely to meet the requirements of our situation. We have an instinctive understanding of what is relevant to our situation. But people also develop careful strategies for advance of their interests, particularly apparent in the support-bargaining directly bearing on the government of a society. Those aspiring to government assess how a national situation may be best presented in order to assemble support for their political advantage. Political organisations focus on the establishment of certain concepts of situation that, being recognised, will assemble support for their cause. Human volition assembles support and drives the political, economic and cultural evolution of human societies.

Yet, for all that, human volition is itself a matter of biological function. The neuroscientific evidence links our psychology to impulses in our brains (Bite 1). So 'up there', in our heads, biological processes take place, of which our volition is simply the manifestation. If it seems that we act from choice, that is only because the biological impulses give it that character. The biological understanding puts a different complexion on the social conception. Social and cultural evolution is probably the same matter of random biological variation and selection as propounded by Darwin, though experienced very differently from the violence that Darwin observed in the process of natural selection. One random variation of supreme importance would be that which gives us the sense of self-preservation and the inclination to seek support, giving rise to group formation. A random variation of similar importance would be that which gives us the capacity to judge our interests by reference to our situation. The best generals judge best the 'lie of the land'; the best politicians judge best how situations can best be presented to their advantage.

That we have the capacity to relate interests and remedial action to situation is plain enough, but how we do it is far from plain. In the simplest cases, we buy a door that fits an aperture by measuring door and aperture; we buy size 12 clothes if we have a size 12 body. But fitting the design and colours of new furniture to an existing décor is not so simple. Selecting transport that will fit the requirements of our situation can be intricate. The suggestion is that we have a sense of symmetry that enables us to perceive patterns in a situation and to discern how additions to the situation will fit into the existing pattern. The precise measurements of doors and clothes are limiting cases of symmetrical fit. We use a sense of symmetry in everyday life to coordinate our performance of tasks. The actions involved in sport, like heading a ball, or parrying a thrust from a foil, require very rapid identification of patterns and reaction to them. Our brains are at least in part symmetry computers, enabling us to perform tasks of 'fitting together' that do not seem feasible if considered in standard mathematical terms. Symmetry is pervasive in the phenomena of the natural sciences, and since we are made of the same stuff as is encountered in the natural sciences, symmetry must play a major role in human behaviour (Bite 28).

Symmetry seems to play a more general role, in that it gives us our sense of 'understanding'. To 'understand' something is to recognise how it fits in with everything else we know. It gives theories, ideas and beliefs that sense of conviction, of grasp, of security, that is the satisfying sense of 'understanding'. By the sense of symmetry, we know when 'things fall into place'. Unfortunately, symmetry is elusive and the human sense of symmetry is fallible. We see symmetry in what we observe when by other measures there is no symmetry; we may miss symmetry when it is present. The same is true of our understanding. False symmetries and a false sense of understanding go together. Ambiguities of perception and understanding reflect inconsistencies of the sense of symmetry.

Bite 4: Social Groups

The pursuit of support leads to the formation of groups. Support is most easily accorded to others when interests are similar, and interests are mostly similar when situations are similar. Hence, groups tend to form amongst people in similar situations. The formation of groups is ubiquitous across societies. They may be small and intimate groups, such as neighbours in a street, or the parents of children at a certain school, or the fans of a village football team. They may be larger groups whose members are not necessarily known to each other but who support one another on the basis of shared interests. 'Engineers' will regard themselves as members of a group on the basis of shared capacities and the shared interest in application of their skills. Owners of a particular model of car may develop a sense of group membership. Residents of a town will conceive themselves as members of the group of townspeople, having a shared interest in the well-being of their town. Groups form over the internet around a great variety of interests, with the members known to each other only through posts on social media.

The archetypal group is the self-forming group, or 'auto-formative group', which determines for itself through internal support-bargaining its defining features, the characteristics or interests on which group membership is based. Fans of Manchester United determine for themselves who meets the criteria for being a member of the group. Members of a group concerned with the conservation of local amenities will determine for themselves which amenities are to be conserved, and how they will be conserved.

This internal support-bargaining to determine a group interest and how it will be pursued gives auto-formative groups an important role in societies. They identify what will be focuses of group attention and hence the issues with which societies will be concerned. All members and aspiring members of a group will have interests that differ at least in some particulars. The formation of a group will involve compromises to identify what will gain the support necessary to build the group and hold it together. The degree of compromise required of each individual member or potential member of the group will be dictated by bargaining positions, centring most importantly on the capacity of a potential member to advance the interests of the group, and the rarity of such capacity. Those with distinctive capacities, skills or qualities most applicable to the emergent interests of the group will find themselves in a position to influence most strongly the group definition of its interest. Auto-formative groups are the forums through which desirable social change can be defined and advanced. Political parties have to take account of the distribution of support in social groups across their societies.

This is also easily understood as the process by which group 'norms' are formed. A group gives its support for certain behaviour and condemns other behaviour. Behaviour in the group becomes constrained to certain acceptable forms. The idea of 'norms' has a central role in the sociological understanding of groups. If someone behaves in a certain way, it is because he or she has assimilated the 'norms' of a group or society. Group membership may be determined by reference to adherence to group 'norms'. People may be regarded as 'middle class', 'working class' or 'patrician' if they behave in accordance with the 'norms' of such groups. The idea of 'norms', however, provides no account of the motivation and interests behind the formation of 'norms'. Support-bargaining explains group behaviour in terms of the pursuit of support.

Auto-formative groups will not entirely determine for themselves their interests and intentions. They will not operate in isolation. Those external to a group, part of the society in which it operates, will influence the internal support-bargaining of the group. Some of those 'outsiders' will wish to divide the group, to deprive it of cohesive support. They will be inclined to impute to the group interests and intentions other than those acknowledged by the group. Those opposed to a particular auto-formative group may try to establish that its interests are detrimental or even pernicious and threatening to the society as a whole. Those concerned with the conservation of local amenities will be challenged by those who seek change. Manchester City fans will not allow Manchester United fans free reign to define the qualities of their team. It is the process of group support-bargaining, a matter of competition to assemble the levels of support that will advance interests. It is an essential element in an open support-bargaining system.

External agents may positively invent or define groups for their own advantage. Such invention includes imputation of interests and intentions to groups whose members may not be aware of being grouped together, and who might repudiate the characteristics imputed to them. The inventions advance the interests of the inventors. Such external group definitions imposed by non-members of the group are invariably designed to condemn the defined group and instigate reactions against it. 'Mondeo man' was a disparaging identification of individuals who belonged to the group defined by ownership of Ford Mondeo cars, thought to be rather boring. The people of English-speaking nations have been classified in French media dealing with political and economic issues as 'Anglo-Saxons', though few English speakers think of themselves in such ancient tribal terms. The implication seems to be that 'Anglo-Saxons' are not to be trusted by honest 'Gauls'. The imposed group definitions impute interests, attitudes and potential actions to the defined group that are likely to impede flows of support to such people, whilst assembling support for groups ranged against them. The 'free market' principles of 'Anglo-Saxons' constitute an ideological threat to the 'dirigiste' approach to economic management favoured in France. The creation of groups by external agencies is akin to the creation of external threats by rulers of a nation state who wish to promote the cohesion of their own group (Bite 6).

External agents also create groups for very specific purposes, though this commonly involves the use of money to secure cohesion. Groups of people are assembled in offices, workshops and factories by business people to undertake prescribed tasks. While this group formation is a requirement of money-bargaining rather than a matter of support-bargaining, it is important to the conduct of societies, since the formation of groups through money-bargaining gives rise to opportunities for the emergence of auto-formative groups. People in workplaces share similar situations and easily form themselves into groups through support-bargaining. These workplace auto-formative groups can reinforce the effectiveness of organisational hierarchies, but can also be detrimental to their functioning. They can also have major political implications. In the nineteenth century, workers were brought together in factories across Europe. The working conditions they encountered prompted auto-formation of groups to pursue improvements, both at factory level and through political support-bargaining. As was seen in Bite 3, the groups organised themselves as trade unions to pursue their objectives more effectively.

The 'norms' of a society referred to above are generally understood as minor behavioural conventions in a society. But the formation of 'norms' through support-bargaining is part of the more fundamental shaping of the distinctive 'culture' of societies, referred to in Bite 2. Societies come to support modes of behaviour that can seem odd and even offensive to people of other societies. 'Clashes of culture' occur within and between nation states. Virtually all societies regard some form of religious belief as of fundamental importance to their way of life; as integral to their social culture. Such belief is woven into the thinking of societies and is reflected in the ceremonies by which they mark births, marriages and deaths. Social culture commonly establishes social hierarchies. Accepted practices are also established with regard to modes of employment—what work is for superior people and what is for inferior, what is for men, what is for women, what is for children. Appropriate clothing is determined by culture. The obligations of parents to their children and the behaviour expected of children are established as culture or 'custom'. Meeting places for social purposes, like pubs in Britain, are established as part of social cultures. Various sports become established as characteristic of cultures.

Cultures change in the face of changing circumstances, though the susceptibility to change and capacity for adaptation are important characteristics of cultures. In violent times, when the survival of societies is at stake, it is recognised that cohesion is essential to survival. Societies faced with the imminent prospect of violent engagement exalt military virtues of loyalty, obedience, conformity, self-sacrifice and courage. Deviance and dissent from established modes of thought and behaviour are condemned. Groups become rigid. Such societies are least able to evolve in response to changing circumstances.

The group rigidity that is the extreme of cohesion is often advantageous in violent action. It is consequently cultivated by those who see advantage in the promotion of violence. Groups may adopt defining characteristics that give them rigidity, or may define groups that are seen as threatening to their interests in rigid terms. Groups defined by reference to ethnicity or ancestry have a rigid character. It is impossible to escape ethnicity or ancestry, so a group defined in such terms is necessarily rigid, in the sense that it is impossible to choose to enter if the criterion for membership is not fulfilled or to escape membership if the criterion for membership is fulfilled. 'Aristocrats' in Britain form a rigid group. 'White people' and 'black people' form rigid groups. 'Eskimos' and 'Jews' constitute rigid groups. While the defining characteristic of such groups is objective, it is a matter of choice that a group is defined in such a way. The political importance of rigid groups is considered further in Bite 6.

Cohesion remains important in a support-bargaining society, even though the extreme of rigidity is associated with violence. A group that easily divides or sheds members over differences concerning what its interests are or how they should be pursued will not be regarded as having the unified support that entitles it to advance of its interests. Support retains psychological implications of violent capacity, so that cohesive support is recognised as significant. Support, vociferous support, united support, conveys messages to others that they should stand down. There is an element of theatre in support-bargaining that conveys to others that a group is cohesive and will not be moved.

While rigidity is one extreme, at the other extreme groups can be very loosely constituted, with a periphery of people who may or may not be members, or who might become members if their interests came under threat, or if other circumstances made it advantageous. Nascent political movements try to 'raise awareness' and raise commitment amongst people who might be expected, from their circumstances, to share the interests of the movement. By calling attention to injustices and asserting that remedies are at hand, support can be assembled that makes a loose group more cohesive and purposeful, and potentially effective in a political support-bargaining process. Such groups may organise themselves as 'pressure groups' or 'interest groups' to pursue interests that cannot be effectively advanced with loosely formed and loosely defined groups.

The looseness of groups is not simply a matter of weak affiliation to any particular group. It involves also affiliations to different groups. People commonly have sympathies with many groups, reflecting their various activities and interests. People live in a certain locality, engage in employment, have leisure activities, pursue their faith and so on. Groups overarch or contain other groups, form sub-groups, and interlock with other groups. 'Oxford people' will include sub-groups of 'university people', 'shopkeepers', 'churchgoers' and 'automotive workers'. Nation states constitute an overarching group membership for most people, with countless sub-groups. Groups 'interlock' when the members of one group are also members of another group, without any prominent overarching group membership. 'Manchester United fans' will be interlocked with 'rich people'. Some Manchester United fans will be rich; some rich people will be Manchester United fans. These interlocks have significance in societies and in their political support-bargaining. If a 'rich person' is also a member of a charitable organisation or faith group, he or she is likely to recognise a wider range of commitments than someone who is just 'rich'. This overarching and interlocking is part of the flexibility in support that makes possible a support convention. The compromises of a support-bargaining system depend on recognition of the competing claims of different interests. Those who have feet in different camps will more easily recognise the claims of the different camps. They will impede the development of the sort of rigidities that lead to violence. Such interlocking memberships can cause people to express opinions in association with one group which conflict with their expressions of opinion when associating with another group. Behaviour may similarly conflict. Commitments to sub-groups may be modified in accordance with changing situations and interests. When the people of a nation state come under external threat, the interests of the overarching national group become prominent. People reconsider their priorities and potentially reassign their support away from a sub-group to the national group.

Bite 5: Organisations

The loose associations commonly implied by the term 'group' are not well suited to the demanding business of 'rule' and the assertion of military force. Groups come together through support-bargaining. When under threat, groups commonly develop high degrees of cohesion. But without external threat, they can fall apart as easily as they come together. A group whose members easily drop their allegiance to pursue their interests elsewhere is limited in what it can achieve.

The effectiveness of groups can be enhanced through organisation. Organisation is used to give group activities a particular focus. It ensures that all involved act in concert to achieve a well-defined purpose. It normally involves the establishment of hierarchical control, exercised by a leader or a group of leaders. Membership of an organised group normally involves assent to the principles established by the group for its management—in particular, the acceptance of a hierarchical role, involving acceptance of direction from those higher up and provision of direction to those below, all under agreed conditions. An individual joining an organisation accepts the right of those at the head of the hierarchy to direct the activities of the organisation towards its settled purposes. The terms of accession to an organisation are much more confining than those involved in joining a group. Individuals generally have much weaker bargaining positions in relation to organisations than in relation to groups.

Groups aspiring to ascendancy in societies before the 'democratic' era were normally obliged to establish a military hierarchy through which control by violence could be exercised when necessary. Ruling groups were often composed of men whose primary affiliation was to a military organisation. Monarchs displayed their military affiliations, implying capacity both for defence of their kingdom against external enemies and for maintenance of civil order.

The control of societies by violence and the threat of violence was tempered most prominently in Europe by religious groups. Such groups formulated ideas of personal morality and ethical behaviour which implied limits on the exercise of violence. The support of these groups for their governments was conditional on the acceptance of such limits. Religious groups could exercise this moderating role because of the extensive support they held across their societies (Bite 2). They too found it expedient to organise themselves for the more effective pursuit of their purpose. While their proclaimed purpose, the purpose around which they assembled their support, was the salvation of souls, the volumes and intensity of support they assembled inevitably gave them social prominence and influence over the conduct of governments and civil affairs. Hierarchies were established that defined what others were to believe regarding the salvation of souls as a condition of entry into the faith group. The heads of religious organisations could also suggest to the ascendant ruling organisations the boundaries of political ascendancy and the consequences in loss of support for overstepping the marks set by them. Their control over the opinions of large numbers within their societies made rulers attentive to their advice. With the intellectual and moral support of religious leaders, rulers could take the measures they desired; without it, they risked erosion of their support in the society. The threat of excommunication by Catholic Popes influenced the behaviour of European monarchs up to the Reformation. The Church of England subsequently became the official religious organisation in

England. It had great influence over the course of events. Even in the twenty-first century, its bishops still sit by constitutional right in the national legislature.

The second essential of effective organisation is the establishment of a money budget. A group can be most effectively organised to a purpose when it is possible to pay members with certain relevant skills for their services. People join a group from commitment to its cause, but if they are to spend substantial time in its service, they must at least be provided with sufficient income to cover the essentials of life. To obtain the most relevant and effective services, it may be necessary to pay rather more. The use of money budgets incorporates incentives of money-bargaining into an organisation. Any discomforts of hierarchy and limitations on opinion and action are compensated by the comforts of relatively secure incomes.

To make these payments, organisations must secure revenues. Monarchs ideally inherited or otherwise appropriated extensive estates, so that their own revenues defrayed much of the costs of their rule. To make up shortfalls, they imposed levies on property and business transactions in their kingdoms. Customs duties were popular, since they were levies on foreign goods and hence apparently on foreigners, and the borders at which such levies could be raised were well defined. It was administratively easy to set up customs posts at ports and border crossings. Taxation of internal transactions was more difficult. Shortly after his conquest of England, William the Conqueror shrewdly surveyed what there was of wealth in the country to determine what his newly established Norman barons and the Anglo-Saxon smaller fry might pay in levies to his exchequer. Budgetary considerations imposed sharp constraints on the behaviour of monarchs, and when the constraints were ignored the results were sometimes disastrous. Aspirations to military glory often tempted monarchs to ignore budgetary constraints. Paying for soldiers and military equipment has always been expensive. Both Charles I in England and Louis XVI in France paid a heavy price for their military adventures.

Governments in the West now receive large revenues from well-developed tax systems. In some countries, state finance is available to political parties aspiring to become governments. But in Britain and the United States, no such finance is available. Parties have to find revenues for themselves to finance their engagement in formal support-bargaining systems. The Conservative Party in Britain spent £16.7 million in the

2010 General Election; the Labour Party spent £8.0 million. The 2016 presidential election in the United States is estimated to have cost the Democratic and Republican parties together a total of $2.3 trillion.

Religious organisations were no less dependent on revenues to sustain their operations. Clergy and staff had to be paid incomes if they were to work full time on church business. Churches, offices and houses had to be built and maintained. The charity identified in doctrine as amongst the foremost of virtues could hardly be exercised without money. The churches found also that, doctrinally improper though it might be, there was much to be gained with regard to social prominence and influence from displays of affluence. People recognised the importance of those who lived and worked in palaces, dressed with elegance and went about in coaches. Those living in penury were treated like everyone else who lived that way. Tithes, payable in cash or in agricultural produce, were a mainstay of the finances of the churches in England. Doctrine also encouraged the faithful to contribute money to their church. The mediaeval Roman Catholic Church in England became very wealthy from bequests of land and property. The wool trade made some mediaeval monasteries wealthy. The dissolution of the monasteries by Henry VIII brought a handsome windfall for a budget under severe stress. Budgetary stress was instrumental in bringing about the great catastrophe of the Catholic Church. To raise the funds necessary for the construction of St Peter's Basilica in Rome, the Church intensified its sales of indulgences. Such sales aroused the ire of Martin Luther and precipitated the fragmentation of Christendom.

Groups concerned with the making of theory have also found it advantageous to form organisations. Religious organisations themselves are established on the basis of theories about the creation of the world and the salvation of its people. Their theories are based on what is recorded in holy books deemed to be inspired by the deity. Monastic orders were established to study the scriptures and learn the will of the deity. The origins of many modern organisations for the formation of theory lie in religious foundations. Such organisations, or institutions, impose hierarchies on their staff. They also establish money budgets for the remuneration of staff and the construction and maintenance of buildings.

Organisation is used to enhance the effectiveness of groups in advancing a focal purpose. The formation of hierarchies and the establishment of budgets mean, however, that other objectives come into play. Heading a hierarchy and controlling a budget imply strong bargaining positions in relation to others both within and outside an organisation. Organisation or institutionalisation produces of itself a new set of opportunities for the advancement of personal interests. Organisation can provide major rewards in the form of hierarchical authority, incomes and opportunities to direct the activities of agencies with strong bargaining positions. Such organisational rewards are sometimes found more attractive than the advance of the focal purpose for which an organisation is established. The 'princes of the church' enjoyed the power and wealth that arose from control over an agency whose extensive support gave it a strong bargaining position across Europe. The salvation of souls was not always apparent as the first priority. Dictators commonly take advantage of their positions to enrich themselves and their families, to the great detriment of good governance in their societies. It is suggested in Bites 12 and 18 that the institutionalisation of learning has had profound effects on the sort of economic theory that has been tolerated.

The use of organisation, with hierarchies and budgets to focus on a purpose, is perhaps most plainly apparent in money-bargaining. Companies constitute organisations formed to focus attention on achieving monetary profits. A company budget is an essential indicator of achievement of the focal purpose. Companies are described in Bite 16.

Notes from the Kitchen

Sources

Bite 1: The Importance of Support
The nature of 'support' and 'support-bargaining' is discussed or recapitulated in all earlier books. Chapter 1 of *Support-Bargaining: The Mechanics of Democracy Revealed* (SBMDR), 'Group Support Bargaining' provides a basic account. Darwin's account of group formation and his treatment of the instinct for self-preservation are discussed in Chapter 1 of *Support-Bargaining, Economics and Society* (SBES), 'The Problem with Natural Selection'. Further, more general, comment on the neglect of the instinct for self-preservation is in the section 'Militarism and self-preservation' in Chapter 7 of SBES.

Darwin discusses human behaviour in Darwin (2004/1871). His biological account of natural selection is Darwin (2009/1859). Darwin was influenced by Malthus (2008/1798). Other references include: Smith (1976/1759), Kaye (1986), and Beer (2008).

A section 'Personification and altruism in sociobiology' in Chapter 8 of SBES discusses altruism. The discussion centres on Wilson (2000/1975) and draws on Kaye (1986), Hamilton (1964), and Dawkins (2006/1976).

Connections between language and support-bargaining are made in SBES, pp. 171–4, drawing on Pinker (1994).

Chapter 6 of SBES assembles 'The Evidence for Support-Bargaining'. The neuroscientific evidence regarding the importance of support derives from Eisenberger et al. (2003), discussed on pp. 27, 49–51, 113–14.

Psychological studies demonstrating the inclination of individuals to conform to group opinions or group norms include Asch (1955, 1956) and Sherif (1935). The formation of 'norms' is easily recognised as an outcome of social support-bargaining (see Bite 4).

Peter Blau emphasises the importance of 'social approval' in Blau (1964). His approach is discussed in *A Theory of Support and Money Bargaining* (TSMB) pp. 11–12, 30–2, 106–9 and in Spread (1984b).

Psychological reactions to perceived threats are described in Kahneman (2012, pp. 301–2). The connection between psychological 'alerts' and the instinct for self-preservation is considered in Chapter 5 of *Economics for an Information Age* (EIA), 'Economics and Behavioural Economics'.

Bite 2: Support-Bargaining: Individual and Group

The dynamics of support-bargaining and the conflict between individual and group are discussed in all earlier books, in varying detail. The opening pages (pp. 9–13) of SBMDR give a basic account. Chapter 2 of SBES, 'Natural Selection and Support-Bargaining', discusses the conflict in a Darwinian context. The discussion draws on Hodgson (1996, 2004) and Wilson (2000/1975).

The conflict between individual and group is discussed in a more modern political context in Chapter 3 of SBES, 'Power and Hierarchy' and Chapter 4, 'Power Elites and Pluralist Democracy'. Chapter 4 draws on literature relating to issues of 'power', including Lukes (2005/1974), Mills (1956), and Bachrach and Baratz (1962).

The conflict has resonated in modern society in rancorous exchanges over 'social Darwinism'. Chapter 7 of SBES, 'Theory Making and Social Darwinism', discusses the issues, drawing on Bannister (1979), Hofstadter (1983/1944), and Crook (1994).

The role of Martin Luther in the support-bargaining that generated the Reformation is briefly commented on in SBMDR, p. 379, and further in SBES, pp. 164–6. The historical background is derived mainly from Guy (2001).

The alliance of church and state in Britain is referred to in *The Evolution of Economies* (TEOE), pp. 121–4. Sources include: Coleman (1977), MacCulloch (2010), and Mokyr (2011). Information aspects of the alliance are covered in Chapter 7 of EIA, 'Media Theory and the Information Interface'.

Cultural affiliations and associated ethnic divisions are mentioned briefly in SBMDR, p. 176. Culture is considered further in Chapter 2 of SBES, 'Natural Selection and Support-Bargaining', esp. pp. 40–51, including comment on Wilson (2000/1975, 2004/1978).

Bite 3: Situation-Related Interest, Social Evolution and the Sense of Symmetry

Situation-related selection is linked with paradigmatic perception and understanding, and to consumer bargaining sets (Bite 15) in TSMB, pp. 58–72. Important references are: Mannheim (1960/1936), Weber (1947/1922), and Lakatos (1970).

Chapter 2 of GIR and Chapter 3 of SBMDR are concerned with situation-related selection, mainly with regard to money-bargaining. The notes to Chapter 2 of *Getting It Right* (GIR) record sources and outline their content. Spread (2011) makes the case for the importance of situation as reference in economic theory. References include: Bruni and Sugden (2007), Earl (1986), Lancaster (1966), and Stigler (1961).

Chapter 1 of TEOE, 'Support Bargaining and the Evolution of Human Societies', recaps on situation-related selection and its evolutionary dynamic (pp. 3–7).

Chapter 10 of SBES, 'Social Symmetries', gives an account of the role of symmetry in social intercourse. The main references are: Stewart and Golubitsky (1992), du Sautoy (2008), and Feynman et al. (1964).

EIA has extensive references to symmetry. Issues of perception and understanding are discussed with reference to symmetry in Chapter 5, 'Economics and Behavioural Economics', and Chapter 7, 'Media Theory and the Information Interface'. In the section 'The symmetry connection' of Chapter 6, symmetry is suggested as a link between the content of our minds and an external reality. Main sources for Chapter 5 include: Kahneman and Tversky (1979) and Kahneman (2012). The sections 'Marshall McLuhan: medium and messages' and 'Poe's follow-up to Innis' of Chapter 7 of EIA discuss McLuhan (1964) and Poe (2011).

Bite 4: Social Groups

Chapter 1 of SBMDR, 'Group Support-Bargaining', includes sections on the 'The formation of groups' and 'The cohesion of groups'. Chapter 10 includes a section on 'The making and impact of socialism'. The section draws on Rose (2002) and Thompson (1991/1963).

The large sociological literature on groups and group 'norms' is discussed in Chapter 4 of TSMB, 'Groups in the Bargaining System'. Important references include: Blau (1964), Chadwick-Jones (1976), Coser (1956), Dahrendorf (1959), Homans (1974), Sherif (1935, 1966), Sherif and Sherif (1969), and Thibaut and Kelly (1959).

Chapter 2 of SBES, 'Natural Selection and Support-Bargaining' is concerned with culture, especially the sections 'The Great Divide: natural selection and cultural evolution' and 'Closing the divide'. Sources include: Wilson (2000/1975, 2004/1978).

Aspects of Support-Bargaining and Money-Bargaining (ASBMB) includes an article, 'The political significance of certain types of group', on the modes of formation and the designation of groups in societies, and their different political implications.

Bite 5: Organisations
Organisations are discussed in Chapter 5 of TSMB, 'Organisations'. Organisation of political parties is described in GIR, pp. 6–7, and SBMDR, pp. 39–40. Chapter 5 of TSMB, Chapter 4 of GIR, and Chapter 4 of SBMDR all describe the functioning of organisations, but mainly in the context of money-bargaining. The principles of organisation in a political context are developed in Chapter 3 of SBES, 'Power and Hierarchy', and in Chapter 4, 'Power Elites and Pluralist Democracy', with sources listed under Bite 2. As noted under Bite 2, relations between church and state are discussed in TEOE, pp, 121–4.

The budgetary problems of Charles I and the emergence of state budgeting are described in SBMDR in a section on 'Stuart finance and the rise of parliament' in Part 5 of Chapter 13, 'Financial Requirements for a Bargaining Society'. The section draws on: Black (1996), Morrill (2001), and Pepys (1997). Louis XVI's budgetary problems are mentioned on p. 396.

The data on election expenditures for the United Kingdom are from The Electoral Commission at http://www.ukpolitical.info/Expenditure.htm. For the United States, it is from the Center for Responsive Politics at https://www.opensecrets.org/.

References

Asch, S. E., 1955, 'Opinions and Social Pressure', *Scientific American*, Vol. 193, No. 5, pp. 31–5.

Asch, S. E., 1956, 'Studies of Independence and Conformity: I. A Minority of One Against a Unanimous Majority', *Psychological Monographs*, Vol. 70, No. 9, pp. 1–70.

Bachrach, Peter, and Baratz, Morton S., 1962, 'Two Faces of Power', *American Science Review*, Vol. 56, No. 4, pp. 947–52.

Bannister, Robert, 1979, *Social Darwinism: Science and Myth in Anglo-American Social Thought*, Temple University Press.

Beer, Gillian, 2008, Introduction to Darwin, 2008/1859.

Black, Jeremy, 1996, *A History of the British Isles*, Macmillan.

Blau, Peter, 1964, *Exchange and Power in Social Life*, Wiley, 1964.

Bruni, Luigino, and Sugden, Robert, 2007, 'The Road Not Taken: How Psychology Was Removed from Economics, and How It Might Be Brought Back', *The Economic Journal*, Vol. 117, No. 516, pp. 146–73.
Chadwick-Jones, J. K., 1976, *Social Exchange Theory: Its Structure and Influence in Social Psychology*, Academic Press.
Coleman, D. C., 1977, *The Economy of England 1450–1750*, Oxford University Press.
Coser, Lewis, 1956, *The Functions of Social Conflict*, Routledge and Kegan Paul.
Crook, Paul, 1994, *Darwinism, War and History*, Cambridge University Press.
Dahrendorf, Ralf, 1959, *Class and Class Conflict in Industrial Society*, Routledge and Kegan Paul.
Darwin, Charles, 2004/1871, *The Descent of Man, and Selection in Relation to Sex*, Penguin. First Published 1871.
Darwin, Charles, 2009/1859, *The Origin of Species by Means of Natural Selection, or the Preservation of Favoured Races in the Struggle for Life*, Sixth Edition, Project Gutenberg Etext, Adobe Digital Editions. First Published 1859.
Dawkins, Richard, 2006/1976, *The Selfish Gene*, Oxford University Press. First Published 1976.
du Sautoy, Marcus, 2008, *Symmetry: A Journey into the Patterns of Nature*, HarperCollins. First Published in Great Britain 2008 as *Finding Moonshine*, Fourth Estate.
Earl, Peter, 1986, *Lifestyle Economics*, St. Martin's Press.
Eisenberger, Naomi, Lieberman, Matthew, and Williams, Kipling, 2003, 'Does Rejection Hurt? An fMRI Study of Social Exclusion', *Science*, Vol. 302, No. 5643, pp. 290–92.
Feynman, Richard P., Leighton, Robert B., and Sands, Matthew, 1964, *The Feynman Lectures on Physics, Volume 1*, Addison-Wesley.
Guy, John, 2001, 'The Tudor Age (1485–1603)' in Morgan, 2001.
Hamilton, W. D., 1964, 'The Genetic Evolution of Social Behavior, I and II', *Journal of Theoretical Biology*, Vol. 7, pp. 1–51.
Hodgson, Geoffrey, 1996, *Economics and Evolution: Bringing Life Back into Economics*, University of Michigan.
Hodgson, Geoffrey, 2004, *The Evolution of Institutional Economics: Agency, Structure and Darwinism in American Institutionalism*, Routledge.
Hofstadter, Richard, 1983/1944, *Social Darwinism in American Thought*, Beacon Press. First Published 1944.
Homans, George, 1974, *Social Behaviour: Its Elementary Forms*, Harcourt Brace Javanovich.
Kahneman, Daniel, 2012, *Thinking, Fast and Slow*, Penguin.
Kahneman, Daniel, and Tversky, Amos, 1979, 'Prospect Theory: An Analysis of Decision Under Risk', *Econometrica*, Vol. 47, No. 2, pp. 263–91.

Kaye, Howard, 1986, *The Social Meaning of Modern Biology*, Yale University Press.
Lakatos, Imre, 1970, 'Falsification and the Methodology of Scientific Research Programmes', in Lakatos and Musgrave, 1970.
Lakatos, Imre and Musgrave, Alan (Eds.), 1970, *Criticism and the Growth of Knowledge*, Cambridge University Press.
Lancaster, Kelvin J., 1966, 'A New Approach to Consumer Theory', *Journal of Political Economy*, Vol. 72, No. 4, pp. 132–57.
Lukes, Steven, 2005/1974, *Power, A Radical View*, Palgrave. First Published 1974.
MacCulloch, Diarmaid, 2010, *A History of Christianity*, Penguin.
Malthus, Thomas, 2008/1798, *An Essay on the Principle of Population*, Oxford University Press. First Published 1798.
Mannheim, Karl, 1960/1936, *Ideology and Utopia*, Routledge and Kegan Paul. First Published 1936.
McLuhan, Marshall, 1964, *Understanding Media: The Extensions of Man*, Routledge.
Mills, C. Wright, 1956, *The Power Elite*, Oxford University Press.
Mokyr, Joel, 2011, *The Enlightened Economy: Britain and the Industrial Revolution 1700–1850*, Penguin.
Morgan, Kenneth O. (Ed.), 2001, *The Oxford History of Britain*, Oxford University Press.
Morrill, John, 2001, 'The Stuarts (1603–1688)', in Morgan, 2001.
Pepys, Samuel, 1997, *The Concise Pepys*, Wordsworth.
Pinker, Steven, 1994, *The Language Instinct*, Penguin.
Poe, Marshall T., 2011, *A History of Communications: Media and Society from the Evolution of Speech to the Internet*, Cambridge University Press,
Rose, Jonathan, 2002, *The Intellectual Life of the British Working Classes*, Yale Nota Bene.
Sherif, Muzafer, 1935, 'A Study of Some Social Factors in Perception', *Archives of Sociology*, Vol. 27, No. 187, pp. 23–46.
Sherif, Muzafer, 1966, *The Psychology of Social Norms*, Harper & Row.
Sherif, Muzafer, and Sherif, Carolyn W., 1969, *Social Psychology*, Harper & Row.
Smith, Adam, 1976/1759, *The Theory of Moral Sentiments*, Clarendon Press. First Published 1759.
Spread, Patrick, 1984a, *A Theory of Support and Money Bargaining (TSMB)*, Macmillan.
Spread, Patrick, 1984b, 'Blau's Exchange Theory, Support and the Macrostructure', *The British Journal of Sociology*, Vol. 35, No. 2. Reprinted in Spread 2015.
Spread, Patrick, 2004, *Getting It Right: Economics and the Security of Support (GIR)*, Book Guild.

Spread, Patrick, 2008, *Support-Bargaining: The Mechanics of Democracy Revealed (SBMDR)*, Book Guild.

Spread, Patrick, 2011, 'Situation as Determinant of Selection and Valuation', *Cambridge Journal of Economics*, Vol. 35, No. 2. Reprinted in Spread, 2015.

Spread, Patrick, 2013, *Support-Bargaining, Economics and Society: A Social Species (SBES)*, Routledge.

Spread, Patrick, 2015, *Aspects of Support-Bargaining and Money-Bargaining (ASBMB)*, e-Book, World Economics Association.

Spread, Patrick, 2016a, *The Evolution of Economies: Money-Bargaining, Economic Change and Industrial Revolution (TEOE)*, Routledge,

Spread, Patrick, 2016b, *The Evolution of Economies: Money-Bargaining, Economic Change and Industrial Revolution (TEOE)*, Routledge,

Spread, Patrick, 2019, *Economics for an Information Age: Money-Bargaining, Support-Bargaining and the Information Interface (EIA)*, Routledge.

Stewart, Ian, and Golubitsky, Martin, 1992, *Fearful Symmetry: Is God a Geometer?* Penguin.

Stigler, G. J., 1961, 'The Economics of Information', *Journal of Political Economy*, Vol. 69, pp. 213–25. Reprinted in Lamberton, 1971.

Thibaut, John and Kelly, Harold, 1959, *The Social Psychology of Groups*, Wiley.

Thompson, E. P., 1991/1963, *The Making of the English Working Class*, Penguin. First Published 1963.

Weber, Max, 1947/1922, *The Theory of Social and Economic Organisation*, Free Press. First Published 1922.

Wilson, Edward O., 2000/1975, *Sociobiology: The New Synthesis*, Belknap Press. First Published 1975.

Wilson, Edward O., 2004/1978, *On Human Nature*, Harvard University Press. First Published 1978.

CHAPTER 3

Political Support-Bargaining

Abstract While individuals have strong concern for self-preservation and tend to shy away from violence, people in groups are more prone to aggression. Support-bargaining within groups, normally under external threat, generates cohesion to the point of rigidity. Rigid groups tend to have violent dispositions. Aversion to the traumas of violence has given rise to adoption of a support convention in many societies, whereby support substitutes for violence. Formal support-bargaining structures are established to give expression to support in the form of votes. Since the larger army can be expected to win a violent encounter, support conventions recognise the authority of majorities. Political parties are organised to assemble majority support across states and within legislatures. The psychological impact of support rests on its association with violent capacity.

Keywords Support-bargaining · Self-preservation · Aggression · Rigid groups · Support convention · Political parties

Bite 6: Aggression and Rigid Groups

As was seen in Bite 1, Darwin's theory of evolution by natural selection emphasised the instinct for aggression as the essential characteristic that made possible the survival of the species. Darwin took his cue from Thomas Malthus, who described tribes as engaged in a 'struggle

P. Spread, *A Starter on Support-Bargaining and Money-Bargaining in Twenty-Eight Digestible Bites*,
https://doi.org/10.1007/978-3-030-05231-7_3

for existence' in the vice of geometric population growth and arithmetic growth in the means of subsistence.

It was suggested also that the emphasis on aggression involved significant underestimation of the significance of the instinct for self-preservation. The individual instinct for self-preservation is, in the understanding of support-bargaining, the instinct that makes individuals feel insecure, driving them to seek the support of associates, and hence to form groups. In general, individuals shy away from violence.

In groups, it is a different matter. Groups have the capacity for effective violence. Security in defence easily metamorphoses into aggressive ambition. There are potentially major rewards from the successful exercise of violence. Territory can be annexed; natural resources can be appropriated; enemies can be subordinated and enslaved. Preponderant capacity for violence makes it possible to exercise control over others. The 'struggle for existence' easily becomes a 'struggle for political ascendancy'—the pursuit of power. Members of a group will give each other support and encouragement. They will recognise the strength that lies in the group. The confidence of the group in its own capacities will grow with the interchange of compliments between its members. Each member of the group will identify an interest in ensuring that others fight for the advantage of the group, and will support those members who show the greatest propensity and capacity for fighting, whilst rejecting those who show no such disposition. Darwin's emphasis on aggression is certainly consistent with the vital role played by physical violence in determining the courses of human societies. The big turning points, the decisive events, in human history are mostly marked by violence. The boundaries of nation states are commonly settled by violence. But it is the violence of groups that is decisive.

The effectiveness of a group in violence depends on its cohesion. A cohesive group can act as if it were a single unit. An army is an organised group, formed to sustain cohesion in pursuit of focal objectives determined by those who create it. Once a group starts to lose cohesion, it loses its effectiveness as a fighting force. The individual instinct for self-preservation reasserts itself. A fighting formation breaks apart and its soldiers run for their individual lives.

The importance of cohesion is reflected in the cultivation of military virtues and military sentiment in virtually all societies. Men need to be of 'the right stuff'. Loyalty is the prime ingredient in the 'warrior codes' of all societies. All nations honour those who have died defending their national territory and way of life. Ideals of patriotism and self-sacrifice are inculcated in children from an early age. The most conspicuous and most honoured acts of altruism are those involving individual sacrifice of life in combat.

Cohesive action is achieved through organisational hierarchy. All in a military organisation are required to obey immediately and without question instructions issued by those above them in the hierarchy. The hierarchy functions like a support-bargaining structure with defined and extreme bargaining positions. Soldiers in a hierarchy have very weak bargaining positions with regard to those above them but very strong positions with regard to those below. Failure to obey orders results in reprimand, incarceration, dismissal from the organisation or even death. There is no room for the flexibility that is apparent in civil support-bargaining. In the circumstances, individual inclination has to be ignored in pursuit of the interests of the group. Hierarchies in civil organisations are of the same kind, though the bargaining positions are less extreme and the sanctions less severe.

Yet, even the inculcation of ideals and the group loyalties that develop within military units are not altogether sufficient to sustain engagement in combat and the cohesion of fighting units over the promptings of the instinct for self-preservation. Most of the millions of soldiers engaged in combat in the twentieth century were conscripts. Armies have quite commonly imposed death by firing squad as the penalty for desertion. The defence of nations required compulsory military service and the enforcement of presence, if not willing cohesion, in the fighting force. Soldiers develop loyalty to comrades in small units, and hence the cohesion necessary to effectiveness in combat. In recent circumstances of limited combat and reduced threats of violence, it has become more acceptable in the West to recognise that the suppression of the instinct for self-preservation in the course of conflict can give rise to acute mental trauma.

Throughout most of human history, contests between violent factions have been the standard means of determining who rules a territory. Control of territory has been of critical importance because of the significance of land to livelihood. Hunting grounds or farmland had to be annexed and protected, and potentially extended. The owners of large estates controlled access to land in their vicinity. Rights to the use of land could be allocated or sold. The necessity of land for subsistence meant that ownership and control of land formed the basis for social and political ascendancy. This importance of land to political order remained right up to the industrial revolution in Europe, when companies gradually became the prime sources of incomes, and hence of livelihood, for many people.

Cultures of violence are ubiquitous. The principles of military organisation are consequently, and almost inevitably, carried over into civil society. Civilians are seen as forming social classes, each with a different 'rank' in the society. In Britain, military officers commonly came from the upper and middle classes of society, whilst the 'rank and file' of the military came from the working class. Civil society required that people 'knew their places', or behaved in a manner appropriate to their social rank. Such social hierarchy in Britain had few sanctions to enforce it other than the prospect of vociferous and hurtful withdrawal of support from those who sought to rise above their allotted place.

Highly cohesive groups, cohesive to the point of rigidity, offer high levels of security to their members. Members do not suffer the confusion of alternative opinion. The commitment to the group cause is shared by all without question. Each group member can be assured of the support of others in any expression of the group opinion. The minimal intellectual demands of rigid groups make them appealing to the less intellectually adroit. There is guaranteed support for anyone who conforms to the commitments of the group.

The security inherent in rigid groups is given prominent expression in the nation state. What were in the earliest times small groups or 'tribes' have amalgamated over the centuries into larger groups, becoming today the nation states that provide a basic identity for virtually all individuals. People think of themselves as French, Dutch, Indian, Chinese, American. They are most at ease on their own territory. Most are more or less ready to fight for their country if it becomes necessary. Many nation states are defined territorially by topographical features, such as rivers, oceans or mountains, that give them defensive advantages. The sense of national identity is inculcated in children from an early age. The process develops confidence, a sense of security and a sense of 'belonging'. Membership of a highly cohesive group, if not a rigid group, seems essential to the human need for security.

The stimulus to the formation of nation states as rigid groups has most prominently been external threats. The tribes and successively larger societies were driven together by the necessity to defend a territory for their survival. Under external threat, the interests of all individuals are tied up with the interests of the group, so that the group readily coheres into an effective fighting force. This effect of external threat on the internal cohesion of groups has often been exploited by rulers to promote cohesive loyalty in their societies. It has even been used to promote the rigidity necessary to expansionary violence. With control of information, external threat can be created as a matter of convenience.

While the rigidity of a nation state gives people a sense of security and confidence, the rigid character of states and the capacity for violence that is inherent in rigidity can excite suspicion and fear in other states. They too then see the necessity of cultivating the rigidity necessary for their defence. Concern over the emergence of external threat will generate external threat. What rigid groups gain from an internal sense of security may be lost through the stimulus they provide to the emergence of rigidity in other groups. This dynamic can be seen in the origins of the First World War.

The security of rigid groups is also apparent in the formation of groups based on supernatural beliefs. In virtually all societies, groups form around ideas of supernatural beings that protect and control them. The inadequacies of human support lead people to invent non-human beings whose support is understood as being of inestimable value to their security and well-being. Great efforts are expended in securing the support of deities. Such ideas permeate whole societies and come to be regarded as incontestable. Anyone questioning them may be physically punished or even killed. The groups are rigid, and like other rigid groups, are ready to fight any who oppose them. The rigidity of faith groups augments fighting capacity. Few armies go into battle without the assurance that 'god' is on their side. Thus, the 'altar' side of a ruling coalition, referred to in Bite 2, can provide social rigidity to reinforce that of the 'throne'.

These religious beliefs—Christian, Islamic, Hindu and many others—are, in the understanding of support-bargaining, sustained by support and thus essentially of the same kind as theories such as 'democratic theory', 'economic theory', or even scientific theory. But clearly in common understanding in most parts of the world, though in Western Europe much less than in earlier times, they have a different status. Theories can be criticised and questioned in a way that is not countenanced with regard to religious belief. The distinction can be attributed largely to the inculcation of religious belief throughout childhood, so that it becomes the foundation of a personal sense of security. Theory assimilated in childhood is generally free from the artificiality that attaches to late-learned theory, in the same way as people speak their native language with less effort than a learned language. Religious belief is so incontestably true to the faithful that it cannot be questioned in a way that is acceptable and even expected with regard to other theories.

In some societies, as noted above, dissent to accepted religious beliefs is brutally punished. Even in more moderate societies, the sensitivity of people to questioning of their religious beliefs has been seen as justifying legislation against such questioning for the protection of social order. People live more quietly and comfortably within the confines of their religious understanding if no one is permitted to raise objections. Religious belief enhances the rigidities of societies. It gives people a sense of intellectual security; of knowing the answers to pressing questions. Religious faith has provided a large measure of the intellectual security that is derived from membership of rigid groups.

The inevitable price paid for such protection is the loss of the flexibility of a support-bargaining system. Rigid groups impede social evolution. If theories cannot be questioned, there is no means by which new ideas can be introduced into a society and bring about change. If the 'situation' is defined in the absolute terms of religious faith, there is no way it can be improved, and no way a society can evolve. In Ireland, rigidities of Catholic belief inhibited social evolution until the Catholic Church lost support as a result of its behaviour over the maltreatment of children. The rigidities of Islamic belief seem to have inhibited the evolution of states in which Islam has a predominant role.

The history of the Soviet Union in the twentieth century displays these features of rigid groups in the context of a secular theory. Karl Marx's theory of communism provided an avowedly rigid and violent understanding of society that was adopted as the intellectual component, the contribution of the 'pen', to the commitments of a violent revolutionary faction wielding its 'sword' against an incumbent ruler. Soviet children were instructed in Marxist theory as diligently as priests had previously provided religious instruction. In the 1930s, Germans voted for fascism to keep out communists. After the Second World War, the proclaimed ambition of the Soviet Union to spread communism around the world brought Western nations together in military alliance. The threat of annihilation of all combatants through the use of nuclear weapons tempered propensities to all-out war. The instinct for countervailing rigidity was nevertheless apparent in the anti-communist campaign against individuals and organisations led by Senator McCarthy in the early 1950s in the United States. Generally, however, the West maintained a commitment to the democratic principle of freedom of expression. The effects of its rigidity were felt most in the Soviet Union itself. The rigid intellectual commitment to Marxist theory made it impossible to acknowledge the true situation brought about by its application. The society could not evolve; could not correct itself. When 'glasnost', 'openness', revealed from 1986 some part of what was going on, the loss of support was terminal.

Bite 7: The Support Convention

Once a nation state has been formed with secure borders, there arises the issue of who is to govern. The faction responsible for establishing the new nation will immediately rule, but inevitably, others will aspire to take over. Violent insurrection has been the traditional means of changing rulers. The governance of most nations through history has been settled by violence between competing factions. Violence was conclusive in a way that no other principle of settlement could rival.

There are, however, severe and obvious drawbacks to the use of violence in the determination of who is to govern, especially if self-preservation is acknowledged as a matter of primary concern amongst humans. The drawbacks seem to have been particularly apparent to English people in the aftermath of the brutal English Civil War of the seventeenth century. There had to be a better way. The traumas of the Civil War made it possible for those involved, and perhaps particularly their children and grandchildren, to adopt less rigid attitudes to monarchy and faith; to become more tolerant. It was found possible to develop a formal support-bargaining system under a 'support convention' whereby levels of support were accepted as conclusive determinants of governing faction. Majorities in parliament rather than armed contests for the crown would determine who ruled. Across Europe, it has been possible to adopt support conventions by which support substitutes for violence for settlement of questions of governance. The Constitution of the United States established a formal support-bargaining system for the governance of the country under a support convention. A support convention provides primarily a means of peaceful determination of which faction will govern a national territory. It then removes the major internal source of violence in a state. Societies take on an entirely new complexion.

There remained, however, in seventeenth-century England and in other European countries, vital issues that could not be settled under a support convention. Landowners would not tolerate the appropriation of their land simply because a majority supported appropriation. As was seen in the previous bite, control of land determined social, political and economic ascendancy. Landowners would fight rather than surrender their property under a support convention. Even the leaders of the parliamentary faction in the English Civil War were landowners and concerned at the potential appropriation of land if the Levellers had their way. Governance had to remain a matter of contest between landowners, and if a support convention was to be used, there had to be protection for their continued ascendancy.

Thus, in early years, support conventions were far from universal. Only the support of those who owned land and property to a certain value was regarded as relevant. The adoption of a support convention was only feasible if restrictions on participation effectively precluded its use for the appropriation of land and property. The adoption of universal suffrage in Britain and the rest of Europe was inhibited for many years by concerns over the potential for redistribution of land and property. 'Land' is also 'territory' and is associated with the exercise of violence. People would fight to protect what they saw as a vital interest. In Britain, something close to universal adult suffrage was established only in 1918, after so many demonstrated the violent counterpart of their support in the First World War. Even the granting of the vote to women over the age of 30, though partly a recognition of the part they played in the war, seems to have been connected to concern over a repeat of the violent demonstrations of suffragettes before the war. Women under the age of 30 years had still to wait until 1928 before they were entitled to vote. The Constitution of the United States, signed in 1787, did not specify who could vote—that was left to the states. In the early years, most states allowed only white male property owners to vote. The nineteenth amendment of 1920 prohibited exclusion from the franchise on grounds of gender.

A vital interest in the southern states of the United States in the ownership of slaves proved beyond resolution through support-bargaining under the terms of the support convention established in the Constitution. In the southern states, slaves were part of the property of landowners. A civil war was fought to establish the conclusive settlement that support-bargaining under a support convention could not provide.

In the years following the civil war, amendments to the Constitution were adopted to facilitate the participation of non-white citizens in formal support-bargaining. But as late as 1964, it was necessary to pass a twenty-fourth amendment to the Constitution to prohibit tax laws designed to prevent non-white citizens from voting.

The progressive extension of the franchise in Britain in the nineteenth and twentieth centuries reflected the diminishing importance of land to political and economic ascendancy. People became increasingly dependent on companies for employment and incomes. The extensions testify also to the effectiveness of support conventions. They have been extended not only with regard to the people whose support is recognised as significant, but with regard also to the variety of issues that can be resolved under them. They have given rise to greater acceptance of compromise in social affairs, a rise in the range of interests that can be at least partially accommodated through political support-bargaining, and a corresponding rise in the number of issues drawn to political attention. Tolerance and reduction in commitments to rigid groups have accompanied the change. The success of the support convention has also led to the development of skills in political support-bargaining, which have in turn been instrumental in its extended use. The involvement of everyone means that most see justification in the use of the convention. People compromise their interests in recognition of the benefits conferred overall.

Nation states are formed to establish territorial boundaries and group identities. Once formed, their political and cultural evolution, including periods of warfare, accentuates their distinct status. Issues between nations are negotiated on a 'quid pro quo' basis, not under a general support convention. External threats have not given the same impulses to group formation amongst groups of nations as they have given to the formation of nation states. There have nevertheless been attempts to create multinational institutions within which the support of each nation is recognised as significant under a support convention. In these institutions, the scope of the convention has had to be limited, just as early support conventions applying within nations had to be limited to take account of the interests of property owners. The significance of support under these limited support conventions is linked to the military capacity of the nation states involved. The most powerful states will not accept determination of issues that affect what they see as their vital interests through a support convention that accords equal status to all nations.

The United Nations has nevertheless provided a forum for oversight of international relations and the implementation of international agreements in areas such as trade, health, weapons proliferation, human rights, child welfare, refugees and environmental protection. It has also provided peacekeeping services to allay violence between and within states.

The European Union is seeking to establish an overarching state of 'Europe' along the lines of a nation state, potentially involving use of an internal support convention over a wide range of issues. The 'support' of significance would be that of individuals as well as nations. The Union originates in part in the desire to avoid armed conflicts between the nation states of Europe, rather than defence against external threat. It has been difficult to achieve the levels of cohesion apparent in nation states. The member states have the rigidity that arises from their origins in defence against external threat and the strong sense of group identity that goes with it. The defence of the Union is not primarily a responsibility of the Union. Defence for the Union and for its individual member states depends principally on the North Atlantic Treaty Organisation, in which the United States is prominent. The multinational state of 'Europe' thus has much less impulse towards cohesion than is apparent in the establishment of most nation states. This deprives it also of the heartfelt sentiment associated with cooperative violence that is a part of national identities. The Union is based on many excellent ideas for the advance of common interests of European nation states, but they are mostly ideas of a cerebral kind that arouse little popular enthusiasm. It is perhaps inevitable that an organisation set up to allay risks of internal armed conflict should fail to inspire the loyalty and commitment that are associated with conflict. The United States, sometimes cited as a model for a 'United States of Europe', fought a war of independence that gave it loyalty and cohesion. The compromises required under a support convention are more easily reached when the overarching group has become cohesive through violent experience.

Bite 8: Formal Support-Bargaining Structures

Governance under a support convention requires a framework in which support can be expressed and enumerated. Societies have created artificial structures for support-bargaining as a means of engaging ordinary people in government in accordance with the principles of democracy. A population is divided into distinct territories, each with roughly the same number of people. Individuals aspiring to represent the people of these constituencies present their programmes, policies, measures and commitments in the hope of assembling the support of constituents. In some systems, whichever individual gains the most support takes a seat in the national legislature. In other systems, seats are assigned to candidates by reference to the proportion of votes received. Measures receiving majority support in a national legislature pass into law.

The structures impose artificial support-bargaining groups on a population. Territorial definition provides clear physical boundaries, and at the same time reflects a fundamental group identity and potentially a group or communal interest. Support-bargaining negotiations are conducted between the members of the defined groups and the individuals aspiring to sit in a legislature. The legislature itself constitutes an artificial forum for the conduct of support-bargaining. Throughout the system, either 'majorities' or 'pluralities' of support are recognised as determinant. A support-bargaining structure gives effect to a support convention. 'Majorities' are acceptable because the larger army normally wins a battle; and if not a majority, a 'plurality' can at least be expected to see off its nearest rival. The structures make possible the engagement of every adult in the support-bargaining that determines the governance of a nation state and the course it takes.

Support-bargaining structures of this kind require that support can be expressed unambiguously and in a form that can be counted. 'Votes' are used to represent support. Votes lack the psychological complexity of support in its basic form, but they serve their purpose. A 'vote' is a distillation or representation of 'support'. It makes no distinction between ardently committed support and support that is little stronger than indifference. As was seen in the previous bite, in earlier times, only the support of those who owned property was regarded as of sufficient importance to be expressed in a 'vote'. Property owners saw themselves alone as having a stake in the country and therefore people who alone could be relied on to protect the country's interests. Their violent capacities and their influence on movements in support deriving from their ownership of property combined to make them the people who made the rules both formally and informally. The reduction of their influence through industrialisation and the proliferation of companies led to extensions of the electoral franchise and finally the establishment of universal suffrage.

To establish majorities for the passage of legislation in a legislature, the individuals elected in constituencies must themselves group together in the legislature. Issues of interest in a particular constituency will not necessarily be shared across other constituencies, so there are no systemic unifying connections between individuals elected to a legislature. Under democratic principles, the members of a legislature debate amongst themselves and a majority emerges for measures that are recognised as conducive to a 'general good'. These might be ad hoc majorities for particular measures proposed to the legislature or majorities for a broader concept of the 'general good' that can be asserted for the advance of numerous measures. Failure to identify a 'general good' in some form leaves democracy at a loss.

Informal support-bargaining has provided a way out of the impasse. Groups in society form with the express purpose of establishing permanent majorities in legislatures for the advance of their interests. Since the formation of sustained majorities has to be based on lasting principles of association and a high degree of cohesion amongst members, these interest groups have organised themselves as political parties. The pursuit of support-bargaining strength in legislatures has brought about the formation of political parties to focus support on particular ideas and interests and establish budgets to finance the assembly of support. The British Conservative Party was originally formed to advance the interests of landowners. As the political significance of this group waned through the industrial revolution, the party became associated with the interests of businessmen. The Labour Party was formed to advance the interests of working people.

The focusing effects of political parties make life easier for ordinary people. Most have limited interest in the minutiae of political issues, limited information about them and limited time to spend on them, so the offer of a broad commitment to pursue certain interests is widely convenient. It is not, in any case, for any individual, worth spending a great deal of time on political issues when a single vote will count for little in the aggregate. People recognise also that their interests will only be significantly advanced if the candidate they vote for becomes part of a majority group in the legislature. Such majority groups will normally be formed by political parties, not by electorally unconnected individuals. Parties are then the focus of practical attention. In some constituencies, a dominant party can effectively nominate who will be the member of the legislature for the constituency. Only the 'marginal' seats are truly contested. Support-bargaining and the support convention have produced structures that are 'democratic', in that they involve large numbers of people in the selection of those who will govern, but are at the same time practical in a way that democracy is not. There is no way that millions of people can 'govern' in any ordinary sense of the word. Organised political parties have sufficient bargaining strength in support-bargaining structures to choose the focus of debate and limit the influence of individuals. Such discounting of highly varied and unorganised individual opinion is essential to the emergence or creation of the majorities that both 'democracy' and support-bargaining require for the determination of what is to be done. A support-bargaining structure nevertheless imposes on political parties the necessity of formulating focal policies that will assemble the support of a significant proportion of a population across constituencies.

Democratic principles use the word 'representative' to describe the relationship between the individual gaining a plurality of support in a constituency with the people of that constituency. The Act of 1918 extending the franchise in Britain was the 'Representation of the People Act'. Other acts pertaining to the electoral structure also use the word 'representation', so in a sense, the meaning of 'representation' is defined in terms of the relationship between elected individuals and the people of their constituency. But the word as commonly used is not appropriate in the political context. Used in the political context, it might be said to express a wish that democratic 'representation' should be 'representation' as commonly understood. Representation implies that the representative shares the opinions of the people and conveys those opinions to external agencies. That would be the democratic ideal. But a candidate winning majority support in a constituency, still more a candidate winning a plurality, is normally opposed by a substantial number. He or she cannot claim to represent all, except in a conciliatory and rhetorical sense. Of necessity, the individuals who vie to 'represent' their constituencies are, if they are representative of any group, representative of their political parties. Virtually any individual seriously aspiring to a seat in the British parliament must first become a member of a political party, implying support for the policies of the party and party support for the individual. They can hardly 'represent' at the same time, in any normal sense of the word, the opinions and interests of a constituency, many of whose people will have voted for someone else. The relationship with constituents is more of a support-bargaining settlement whereby the aspiring individual undertakes to deliver the policies and programmes adopted by a political party to the constituency members, if the party achieves a majority in the legislature, in exchange for a plurality of support received from them.

A candidate may similarly be seen as establishing an agreement through support-bargaining with a political party, rather than 'representing' it. The candidate undertakes to support the party in the legislature in exchange for the support of the party for his or her efforts to assemble support in a constituency. The affiliation is vital to candidates because of the functions of parties in presenting easily assimilated focal policies and in forming legislative majorities, as described above. The theory of support-bargaining provides explanations of observable processes that are left hanging in democratic theory.

Bite 9: Political Parties

Political parties are easily seen as the successors to the violent factions that contested government in earlier times in Europe. Military effectiveness required the hierarchies and funding that came with organisation. Political parties in a formal support-bargaining system, operating under a support convention, have no lesser requirement for the advantages brought by organisation (Bite 5). Support substitutes for violence, but organisational advantages are common to both the exercise of violence and engagement in support-bargaining.

Engagement in formal support-bargaining under a support convention nevertheless imposes great changes on political parties. Under a support convention, the skills in demand are not those of military leadership or prowess with a sword. The emphasis is more on ideas and facility in debate. Information and ideas conducive to the interests of the party have to be disseminated in such a way as to raise support amongst citizens. The information and ideas purveyed by opponents have to be confounded by argument. Persuasive capacities, linguistic fluency, rhetorical skills and facility with ideas are important qualities. Expansion of education services has accompanied the expansion of support-bargaining systems, so that people in general are better able to understand and judge the implications of ideas and are at the same time inclined to allocate their support to those propounding ideas they favour.

As was seen in the previous bite, political parties must also adapt to the exigencies of the formal support-bargaining structure. This has naturally meant adaptation to formal support-bargaining structures as they have evolved, from very restrictive participation to universal adult participation. The purpose of political parties in parliamentary systems has been the formation of majorities in a legislature. This means success in constituencies across a nation. There is a requirement for focal policies that will assemble support all across a country. In support-bargaining structures with limited participation, money and 'treats' could be more effective than policies in assembling support. With a universal support convention, political parties must assemble support across nations on the basis of focal policies and commitments that have extensive appeal. There is a requirement also for organisation at constituency level to run campaigns that are attentive to local interests and can bring out local support. The old violent factions assembled support across their territories by alliances with local lords, often through family connections.

While support-bargaining under a support convention suggests increased emphasis on the importance of ideas in the assembly of support, the dispositions of ordinary people mean that the social allegiances that played such a prominent part in the old 'calls to arms' may be just as important, perhaps more important, than ideas. Something like the group loyalties and communal affiliations that sustained the old factions remain essential to the assembly of support for political parties contesting election in formal structures. A broad commitment to pursuit of certain interests will be enough to determine the allegiance of many voters. Both Conservative and Labour Parties in Britain derive some of their support from traditional affiliations based on social class.

Hierarchy was identified in Bite 3 as an essential element in the effectiveness of organisation. In military organisations, hierarchies run through many levels, from Chief of General Staff down to private soldiers. Political parties have not found it necessary to create extended hierarchies. They try, nevertheless, to appoint able people to lead short chains of command, both to shape the party's focal commitment and coordinate the various tasks involved in the assembly of support. They try also, as a matter of the highest priority, to appoint a personable, preferably charismatic, leader who will draw support to the party. While ordinary people have limited interest in the minutiae of political policies, their attention may be drawn to a personable leader. Policies may be abstruse and demanding, but personality is a matter of ready reaction. Given that, in an age of electronic communications, political messages have to be communicated through the media, a leader has to have media skills and the sort of 'screen presence' that is associated with film stars.

The importance of leadership affects the tussle between the individual and the group, described in Bite 2 as lying at the heart of support-bargaining. For some political parties, there are compromises to be made. Parties of the left are committed to the ascendancy of the group over the individual. Concessions to a leader, even if he or she offers potential advantages to the party with regard to assembly of support, run contrary to the basic principles of the party. The internal support-bargaining structure of the British Labour Party dispersed authority over the appointment of a leader across trade unions, the rank and file of the party and Labour members of parliament. Even so, in the 1990s, a faction of the party, anxious that it should be a party of government after an extended period of Conservative rule, succeeded in gaining the adoption of Tony Blair as leader. 'New Labour' accepted major compromises with regard to the ascendancy of the group, both in terms of party structure and in the policies it would present to the electorate. Sure enough, under Blair's leadership, the party won three general elections in succession. After the election of Ed Miliband as leader, a new system was introduced which took the party back to its group convictions.

In the Conservative Party, compromise took a different form. The formation of a party to pursue individualism seems almost a contradiction in itself. The group will necessarily erode the individualism. But without the group and the organisation of a party, the individual interest would go begging, so the individual interest has to be reconfigured as a group interest. Issues of leadership are much less contentious in such an organisation. 'Leadership' is cultivated as part of the individualist conception of society. Before 1965, it was held that leaders of the Conservative Party 'emerged' naturally amongst party members, meaning that leaders emerged from internal informal support-bargaining. Those ascendant in the Party determined who the leader would be. After the 'emergence' of Sir Alec Douglas-Home as leader, to the surprise of many leading figures in the party, it was determined that the leader should be appointed by its members of parliament. Edward Heath was the first beneficiary of the new system. Involvement in selection was later extended to members of constituency parties. The Party moved from a quasi-authoritarian individualism to a more 'groupie' approach to the selection of its leaders, in the expectation of appointing leaders who would be more effective in assembling support from an electorate whose interests were shaped by industrial employment.

Donald Trump perhaps exacted the greatest concessions from the party in his accession to the leadership of the Republican Party in the United States. The charisma of Trump, previously in evidence as host of a 'reality television' show, and radical popular policies, attracted extensive support, first in the Republican primary elections through which he won the leadership of the Party, and subsequently in the presidential election of 2016. The use of primary elections for the selection of leaders makes it easier for a party to select an individual and his policies in preference to the established policies of the party than in the more restricted systems used for the appointment of British party leaders. The 'concessions' of the established top dogs of the Republican Party hierarchy were forced upon them by demonstrations in the primaries of Trump's effectiveness in raising support.

The use of primary elections in the United States may be seen as an adaptation of political parties to a particular system of formal support-bargaining. Accession to government in the United States involves not just, or even essentially, the establishment of a majority in a legislature, but winning the constitutional position of president. Presidential elections put an individual in the electoral spotlight more than parliamentary elections. Parties use primary elections as a means of identifying an individual who can potentially win a presidential election. Trump is nevertheless unique in having, in the course of his accession to the leadership, forced on an established party policies and commitments that had limited support within its established hierarchy.

The organisation of a political party involves the establishment of a party budget. Effective participation in formal support-bargaining involves the expenditure of large sums of money on dissemination of information about party positions, on movement of party members around the country and on employment of campaign staff. As was seen in Bite 5, in some countries, provision is made for government funding of political parties. Such provision recognises that, under democratic principles, monetary expenditures should not influence the outcome of elections. In other countries, including Britain and the United States, parties must raise their own revenues. Any influence of donors on the policies adopted by parties is regularly denied by party officials, but given the importance of finance, donors must necessarily be amongst those who influence the policies that parties choose to make prominent. The media in Britain report from time to time that a donor has withdrawn, or threatened to withdraw, a contribution unless party policy is changed.

While the use of money to advance electoral interests is incompatible with democratic principles, so too are political parties. Political parties give power to party leaders and their associates. They develop strong bargaining positions that enable them to advance their own concerns and their own concepts of how society should evolve. 'The people' participate in accordance with democratic principles through formal support-bargaining structures, but political parties govern.

Notes from the Kitchen

Sources

Bite 6: Aggression and Rigid Groups

Extensive reference is made to the rigidity and flexibility of groups in earlier books, since these characteristics of groups are of central importance to the character of societies. Chapter 4 of *A Theory of Support and Money Bargaining* (TSMB) includes a section on 'Social significance of interlock of groups', drawing on: Dahrendorf (1959), Coser (1956), and Blau (1964).

The significance of the instinct for self-preservation and the influence of Thomas Malthus (2008/1798) are discussed in Chapter 1 of *Support-Bargaining, Economics and Society* (SBES), 'The Problem with Natural Selection'. Chapter 2 includes a section on 'Violence and rigid groups'. Nations as rigid groups and questions of vital interests are explained on pp. 39–40. A section of Chapter 5 discusses 'Rigidity of kin groups'. Chapter 8 discusses religious faith (pp. 162–8), with a section on 'Deity theory and common theory'.

Chapter 5 of *Getting It Right* (GIR), 'Support-Bargaining', and Chapter 1 of *Support-Bargaining: The Mechanics of Democracy Revealed* (SBMDR), 'Group Support-Bargaining' both include a section on 'Rigid groups'. *Aspects of Support-Bargaining and Money-Bargaining* (ASBMB) includes an article, 'The Political Significance of Certain Types of Group', which explains the political importance of rigid groups. References are appended.

Territory and property are discussed in the context of the evolution of economies in *The Evolution of Economies* (TEOE), pp. 108–9, 118–21. Important references are: Coleman (1977), Thompson (1991/1963), and Gillingham (2001).

The decline in the importance of land and landowners and the rise in the importance of companies as sources of the necessities of life is a major theme of Chapter 5 of TEOE. The use of violence in foreign trade is covered in Chapter 6 on 'The Evolution of Foreign Trade'.

Bite 7: The Support Convention

Chapter 13, Parts 2 and 3, of SBMDR, 'Human and territorial boundaries: the defining group' and 'Changing character of groups in an emergent bargaining society', describe the formation of nation states. Part

4 of the same chapter, 'Emergence of the support convention', gives a brief account of the historical development of a support convention in Britain. Sources include: Morgan (2001), Black (1996), and Thompson (1991/1963). The Conclusion of SBMDR has a section on 'The European Union'.

Chapter 2 of SBES includes sections on 'Natural selection and the support convention' and 'The support convention in practice'.

Bite 8: Formal Support-Bargaining Structures
Chapter 2 of SBMDR, 'Formal Support-Bargaining' describes electoral systems as bargaining structures and the role of political parties operating in the structures. Ideas of 'democracy' and their shortcomings are based on Roberts (2000) and Dunn (2005), drawing also on McKenzie (1964) and Wildavsky (1979).

Chapter 5 of GIR has a section on 'Representation of political parties'.

Bite 9: Political Parties
Chapter 5 of TSMB, 'Organisations', analyses the function of organisations in both support-bargaining and money-bargaining. The chapter starts with consideration of political parties and their compatibility with democratic principles. Sources include: Birch (1973) and Blondel (1963).

Chapter 2 of SBMDR has a section on 'Political parties in the formal structure'. Sources include Roberts (2000). Chapter 13, Part 7, is concerned with 'Leaders in Bargaining Societies'.

Joseph Schumpeter's (1994/1942) contention that democracy is a contest between individuals for power is discussed in a section of Chapter 3 of SBES, 'Individuals and groups: the Schumpeter theory of democracy'. The Conclusion to SBES provides further comment on individual leadership (pp. 256–7).

References

Birch, A. H., 1973, *The British System of Government*, Allen & Unwin.
Black, Jeremy, 1996, *A History of the British Isles*, Macmillan.
Blau, Peter, 1964, *Exchange and Power in Social Life*, Wiley.
Blondel, Jean, 1963, *Voters, Parties and Leaders*, Pelican.
Coleman, D. C., 1977, *The Economy of England 1450–1750*, Oxford University Press.
Coser, Lewis, 1956, *The Functions of Social Conflict*, Routledge and Kegan Paul.

Dahrendorf, Ralf, 1959, *Class and Class Conflict in Industrial Society*, Routledge and Kegan Paul.
Dunn, John, 2005, *Setting the People Free*, Atlantic Books.
Gillingham, John, 2001, 'The Early Middle Ages (1066–1290)', in Morgan, 2001.
Malthus, Thomas, 2008/1798, *An Essay on the Principle of Population*, Oxford University Press. First Published 1798.
McKenzie, R. T., 1964, *British Political Parties*, Heinemann.
Morgan, Kenneth O. (Ed.), 2001, *The Oxford History of Britain*, Oxford University Press.
Roberts, David (Ed.), 2000, *British Politics in Focus*, Causeway Press.
Schumpeter, Joseph A., 1994/1942, *Capitalism, Socialism and Democracy*, Routledge. First Published 1942.
Spread, Patrick, 1984, *A Theory of Support and Money Bargaining (TSMB)*, Macmillan.
Spread, Patrick, 2004, *Getting It Right: Economics and the Security of Support (GIR)*, Book Guild.
Spread, Patrick, 2008, *Support-Bargaining: The Mechanics of Democracy Revealed (SBMDR)*, Book Guild.
Spread, Patrick, 2013, *Support-Bargaining, Economics and Society: A Social Species (SBES)*, Routledge.
Spread, Patrick, 2015, *Aspects of Support-Bargaining and Money-Bargaining (ASBMB)*, E-Book, World Economics Association.
Spread, Patrick, 2016, *The Evolution of Economies: Money-Bargaining, Economic Change and Industrial Revolution (TEOE)*, Routledge.
Thompson, E. P., 1991/1963, *The Making of the English Working Class*, Penguin. First Published 1963.
Wildavsky, Aaron, 1979, *Speaking Truth to Power: The Art and Craft of Policy Analysis*, Little Brown.

CHAPTER 4

Intellectual Support-Bargaining

Abstract 'Intellectual support-bargaining' is support-bargaining for the assembly of support around ideas and theories that are likely to advance the interests of their formulators. Adoption of a support convention increases the dependence of a society on ideas. Theories function as frames of reference, directing attention to certain phenomena and promoting interpretations sympathetic to the interests of the theorists. Theory formation has been institutionalised in universities as the pursuit of truth. Procedures to reduce the impact of non-truth interests have been adopted most prominently in the natural sciences, where the relative stability of the phenomena makes them amenable to such procedures. The theory of support-bargaining provides a frame of reference by which the phenomenon of theory-making itself can be recognised and explained. It provides a 'frame of frames'.

Keywords Intellectual support-bargaining · Theory formation · Frames of reference · Narrative · Support convention · Scientific method

Bite 10: Common Theory

Social support-bargaining establishes social groups and in the process establishes common ideas about the nature of the world and its people. The emergence of ideas and theories in the course of support-bargaining

P. Spread, *A Starter on Support-Bargaining and Money-Bargaining in Twenty-Eight Digestible Bites*,
https://doi.org/10.1007/978-3-030-05231-7_4

is usefully distinguished from other political and social support-bargaining as a process of 'intellectual support-bargaining', although the three spheres of support-bargaining are always closely linked. Support assembled in one sphere registers in others. 'Ideas', 'theories', 'opinions', 'sentiments', 'propositions', 'policies' and so on are not sharply distinguished. The concept of 'intellectual support-bargaining' is of most advantage in distinguishing the process by which more sophisticated theories are developed, mostly amongst specialist theory makers. In that context, it is usually the preserve of people noted for their intellect and set apart in institutions for the specific purpose of forming theories for the guidance of social and political action.

Nevertheless, it is useful also to distinguish a similar process amongst ordinary people whereby a common theory is formulated for the guidance of everyday behaviour. Common theory provides group understanding of the world and its people sufficient to enable them to go about their daily business with reasonable assurance of things turning out as they expect and ensuring they remain in good standing with those around them. Common theory gives people an understanding of how they should conduct themselves in their community. It makes people aware that if they are offensive to someone, they are likely to be punished in some way, perhaps by retaliation from the offended person, or by the condemnation of the community. Common theory also provides an understanding of the nature of the phenomena encountered in the natural world. Seeing a tree is understood as seeing something that exists independently of the sighting of it. Events can be understood in terms of causation. Wind causes fences to fall. Water causes timber to rot. Where there is no readily identifiable cause, people may create causal agencies whose presence is adequately confirmed by the effects attributed to them. Not so long ago, if the milk went sour or a knife went missing, it was regarded as the work of 'fairies', 'gremlins', or some other fanciful beings with benevolent or malicious inclinations towards humans. Such 'folklore' provided acceptable explanations of events that were otherwise inexplicable. In general, people prefer some explanation, however fanciful, to no explanation.

Some content of common theory derives from the more sophisticated realm of intellectual support-bargaining. Theories of supernatural causation have been developed in all societies, usually originating from people regarded as set apart from the common order. Such theories have been adopted amongst ordinary people, to an extent that makes them part of common theory. Whole societies commonly become infused with a particular theory of supernatural causation. The theories accumulate such support that, as was seen in Bite 2, their proponents become engaged in the process of government. Such is the close linkage between intellectual and political support-bargaining. The commitment to such theories has meant that they have been organised and institutionalised, with hierarchies and budgets, giving them a prominent and durable role in their societies. In all societies, they provide a major focus of cohesion. As part of their lore, they invariably provide a kind of external threat—the threat of divine retribution—that is conducive to conformity and cohesion. While deity theories over centuries in Western Europe held such a hold on the minds of ordinary people that they have to be regarded as part of common theory, their modern status is not so secure. Many people still find consolation in distress from religious teaching, and many follow its precepts of behaviour, but unquestioning faith in its absolute truth is probably less common.

The support inherent in common theory establishes boundaries to what is feasible in political support-bargaining. The historical support for commitments of faith gave religious orders their influence over government. Governments could do only what well-supported religious orders found tolerable. Overstepping such marks risked loss of the support that maintained their rule. Similarly, ideas of individual entitlements, family responsibilities and communal obligations established in common theory place constraints on the actions open to political leaders if they are to maintain support. Common theory represents reservoirs of support for various social commitments which can be drawn on for political purposes and can seldom be ignored without adverse consequences.

Many find the explanations of common theory inadequate. Questions about why milk goes sour or knives go missing, or why some things float on water and others sink, or why the sun rises every morning, are not satisfactorily explained for everyone in common theory. People have sought other explanations. While the religious elements of common theory derive from more sophisticated theory making, many other matters of sophisticated theory making have their starting points in common theory. Much institutionalised intellectual support-bargaining is concerned with issues of common theory. Institutions of learning around the world have been established to investigate common events and behaviour. Social scientists—sociologists, economists, psychologists, etc.—have shaped theories about human behaviour. Natural scientists have identified elaborate chains of causation relating to material things. Philosophers have probed the logical foundations of human understanding, questioning even the supposition in common theory that seeing a tree confirms the existence of a tree.

'Common theory' is not normally classified as theory at all. There are common ideas and common notions; there is a popular 'mindset'. There are beliefs about various influences on material and human affairs. There is a 'populism' that influences political support-bargaining. But these are not regarded as warranting classification as 'theory'. Proper 'theory' is understood as something formulated by a notably intelligent section of the community in the confines of institutions set up for the purpose of discerning 'the truth' about the world. It is systematically formulated through debate and testing within the institutions. What survives the process is retained as true theory; what fails the tests is discarded.

In support-bargaining, theory formation is understood as part of an overall process of assembling support for the advance of interests. Since people will support ideas, and such support is often given also to related proposals for political action, the formation of ideas, or theory, is part of the process by which interests are advanced in a society. Common theory influences political action. Institutionalised theory making is similarly concerned with the advance of interest. While practitioners proclaim their intention to pursue the truth as a matter of universal interest, that is not necessarily the only or even the first priority (Bites 5, 28). Support-bargaining is used in the creation of both common theory and institutional theory. The formation of common theory has the same dynamic as the formation of institutional theory. While institutional theory formation is more consciously systematic, common theory is not entirely lacking in system. Much of it is sustained by observation and experience. Much of its content is tested multiple times by multiple agents. It permits societies to function and sustain themselves. Common theory most conspicuously lacks system in its adoption of supernatural theory, but much of that derives from institutionalised theory makers.

The conviction attaching to common theory derives largely from assimilation in childhood. Early assimilation gives it that quality of being self-evident and incontestable which is generally lacking in late-learned theory. It is partly this feature also that distinguishes it from most of the theory formed in formal institutions, and consequently makes it easier to regard common theory as something other than proper 'theory'. People assimilating the same ideas in childhood find it easier to support one another in adult life and maintain social cohesion. As was seen in Bite 6, religious faith also is not commonly regarded as theory. It too is mostly assimilated in childhood and has the quality of theory learnt at that early stage.

Institutional theory makers necessarily assimilate the common theory of their society in childhood, so that although they may not recognise common theory as 'proper' theory, they nevertheless use it extensively and ceaselessly. Theory makers, however scholarly, cannot entirely escape from the society that surrounds them. Of necessity they use a language developed for communications based on common theory. Much of what is written is effectively an appeal to 'common sense'. Common observation and common experience are largely taken for granted. Academic writers make frequent reference to received opinion, sometimes referring to the received opinion of a specialist group, but sometimes to the common theory of society at large. Common theory underpins much academic speculation in the way that it underpins also the conduct and opinions of ordinary people. Institutional theory extends and may contest common theory but is not independent of it.

Assimilation of common theory in childhood can be regarded as a matter of intellectual support-bargaining. Much of the behaviour of children can be seen as support-bargaining or the learning of support-bargaining. But children have such weak bargaining positions as to differentiate the process quite sharply from that of adult intellectual support-bargaining. Children are dependent on adults for their physical and mental well-being. Children are instructed in common theory and admonished when they get it wrong. They have to 'do as they are told' or suffer punishment. Children's minds are in process of formation, so they are more susceptible to outside influence than adults.

One favoured means of communicating common theory to children is through 'stories'. 'Stories' impose something of the status of 'reality' or 'real life' on imaginative invention. They 'bring to life' imagined events. They make it easy to assimilate the ideas and instructions they contain. The supernatural elements of common theory, and the guidance they imply, are commonly conveyed to children through 'stories'. They give children the equivalent of what in the more sophisticated context of institutional learning are described as 'frames of reference' (Bite 12). Stories give children a basis for observation and understanding of the behaviour of people around them. They provide also the sense of security enjoyed by theory groups that share a frame of reference. Even in the sophisticated context, theorists have adopted the idea of 'narrative' as something akin to a 'frame of reference'.

Stories in the form of myths, fables and parables commonly convey instructions or messages about what constitutes good conduct in a society, how people should behave towards one another, and what happens to people whose behaviour is contrary to what is expected of them. Wicked witches and sinners come to bad ends. They provide guidance also on gender relationships and the significance of material wealth. 'True love' triumphs over the machinations of the mercenary. They have been major means of assembling support across societies for ideas of 'morality' and 'ethics'. They define acceptable behaviour in a form readily assimilated and not easily forgotten. They introduce children to the settlements established through support-bargaining between individuals and their societies. The children of the digital age will have more voluminous and diverse sources of instruction than those of previous generations.

In the Western world, the most influential stories have been those of the Bible. Christian morality and ethics have been assimilated by successive generations through biblical parables, forming a major part of common theory. Even without the underlying faith, the stories are still recognised as usefully instructive. Other societies have similarly recorded stories in books that are regarded as deriving in some way from divine authority. Deities are presented as teaching their humans how to conduct themselves, both towards each other and towards the deities, through the medium of stories.

Bite 11: The Support Convention and Intellectual Support-Bargaining

In the conduct of national affairs, efforts to advance interests have historically been strongly influenced by the potential for settlement by violence. Violence has a finality that is attractive to those with preponderant capacities for violence. The finality of duels was used to settle personal disputes in Europe into the early years of the nineteenth century. The establishment of a support convention in a nation state ostensibly rules out violence as a means of settlement. Attention then transfers to ideas, policies and programmes, and the persuasive arguments that will assemble support. Intellectual support-bargaining becomes much more prominent and decisive in the conduct of the affairs of a nation.

In Europe, this has meant intensification of the institutionalised pursuit of understanding of human societies and human behaviour. Ideas of earlier ages were largely limited to those of faith groups shared in essence across a society, if contested in detail. The new requirements gradually moved institutionalised learning away from its commitments to religious themes and towards secular speculation over the principles and practicalities of the conduct of nation states. Theories were developed regarding the 'democratic' conduct of societies and the desirability and feasibility of various economic relationships that might be promoted by the state or emerge spontaneously amongst the people of a state.

The process of theory formation was understood as a search for 'truth' in some absolute sense, in the way that deity theories have been understood as presenting 'the truth' about the human condition. Theories are, however, more consistently explained as being consciously or unconsciously constructed for the advance of the interests of the groups that formulate the theories. Rulers in particular, especially when conceived in terms of a ruling group, or 'ruling class', generally had an interest in the adoption amongst their people of theories that justified the existing order. That interest was apparent in the formulation of much deity theory. Monarchs claimed to rule by divine right. Secular theories that assembled support for existing rule were favoured by rulers, but secular theories of different import were favoured by groups opposed to the ruler or the ruling class. Theories that seemed more transparently formulated to advance the interests of particular groups, as opposed to the pursuit of truth or the pursuit of universal advantage, came to be referred to as 'ideologies'. The 'ideologies' were invariably formulated by those who aspired to rule. Theorists sympathetic to the rulers successfully imposed on the 'ideologies' negative connotations of manipulation for the advance of factional interests, thus impeding their accumulation of support.

Ideas of 'democracy' initially fell into the category of 'ideology'. The ideas were reviled by the ruling classes across Europe as constituting nothing more than 'mob rule' that would potentially appropriate their land and property. But the accumulation of support for such ideas was so extensive that they came to be recognised not perhaps as sound theory, being much less comprehensive in their coverage of political affairs than was desirable in a theory, but at least as excellent principles on which to base a system of government. They might be 'ideological' in advancing the interests of ordinary people, but the extent of the support accumulating around them effectively lifted them from the unappealing status of 'ideology' to something more like sound theory. 'Ideologies' remained the term used for ideas that sought in a more distinctly partisan and robust manner the overturn of the ruling classes.

The increased recognition of the role of ideas in the assembly of support meant an increased recognition of the importance of those skilled in the analysis of information and the formulation of ideas and theories. Whereas the intellectual elite, such as it was, had previously been associated largely with faith groups, a new intellectual elite emerged based on skills with secular information. Specialists in academic institutions increasingly took responsibility for theory formation, with the assurance that their isolation placed them in a position from which they could truly pursue 'the truth', untrammelled by the everyday interests that were likely to distort the theories of everyone outside. On this assurance, they were frequently invited to advise governments on civil, military, international, economic and social affairs. Academic institutions became centres of intellectual support-bargaining for the accumulation of support around theories relating to the conduct of their societies.

In recognition of the growing importance of skills in the assembly and analysis of information, and the rapidly growing range of subjects in which governments were expected to play a part, permanent advisory services were established as adjuncts to government. These 'civil services' engage internally in intellectual support-bargaining to identify best courses of action relative to the situations which a nation experiences. The outcomes of these internal debates have a major bearing on what is done in the name of governments. Civil servants gain relevance from their involvement in day-to-day decision-making that is potentially lost to those formulating theory in the isolation of academic institutions. Civil servants will deal with real situations and immediate events, whereas the situations conceived in academic institutions tend to be more general and abstract.

A more public form of intellectual support-bargaining is apparent in the news media. The information that reaches ordinary people about the problems and decisions of governments is largely derived from newspapers and electronic media, including now the internet. The internet gives unprecedented opportunities for ordinary individuals to circulate information, but still the major debates centre on information communicated through organised news media with large audiences. Proprietors, editors and journalists who compile media reports are engaged in the assembly of support through the arguments and 'stories' they publish. At the very least, they select what issues will be brought to the attention of readers, listeners and viewers. Beyond that, there is ample scope in language for the manipulation of information in such a way as to assemble support for the advance of favoured interests.

Most of the organised media are constituted as companies, so that their overriding concern is the pursuit of monetary profit. They are primarily money-bargaining agencies, rather than support-bargaining agencies. The interest colours the issues they select for presentation and the way they are presented. While a profit-oriented media interested also in advancing certain favoured interests is unlikely to disseminate the sort of information that might ideally be provided as the basis on which ordinary citizens would allocate their support, and hence determine the political course of a nation, the saving grace is the availability of multiple sources, not all favouring the same interests. The internet has in recent decades greatly expanded alternative sources of information and opinion. There remain, however, in Britain, prominent media organisations that have a major influence on the support that citizens accord to political parties and interests. Bite 27 considers further the role of media as purveyors of information in bargaining societies.

The adoption of a support convention involves an emphasis on assembly of support for ideas and theories. Such assembly requires that people are free to express their ideas and opinions. Hence, the idea of 'free speech' is accepted as an essential part of 'democratic' societies. Yet, support-bargaining implies constraints on what people say. Denial of support, more or less forcefully expressed, constitutes informal censorship in a support-bargaining society. People who say the 'wrong' thing or who express certain opinions will be denied support and accordingly denied the sort of advancement that goes with assembly of support. This denial of support is expressed formally through legislation. There are laws against libel, propagating false information, threatening behaviour and incitement to violence. Support-bargaining societies tend to impose formal restrictions on expression that threatens to take social and political relationships beyond the bounds that are acceptable under a support convention—that is, expression likely to give rise to violence.

Under a support convention, levels of support dictate the advance of interests. The formation of like-minded people in groups is thus of central importance. People of similar interests, who tend to be people in similar situations, form groups to advance their interests. The support-bargaining process gives rise to the formation of group opinion and group 'solidarity'. While people positively see opportunities for the advance of their interests by giving their support to a group, they will also fear the isolation that arises from lack of support from associates. There is consequently inclination to accept the settled opinion of the group. The opinions of everyone are influenced by the necessity of group support, but those least secure in the group, having the least settled support, are most likely to accept the opinions of the group. The least secure are generally those who have least to offer the group in terms of expertise or talent relevant to the group interest.

This intellectual support-bargaining lies behind the phenomenon of 'groupthink', so named by Irving Janis in 1972 in the context of analysis of decision-making over the abortive 'Bay of Pigs' invasion of Cuba under President Kennedy and other events. In the understanding of support-bargaining, all 'think' is 'groupthink'. Everyone's thought is influenced by the necessity of retaining support amongst their associates. Being isolated, without support, is the worst circumstance. Thoughts are moulded to the requirements of human association. People 'come to terms' with their associates. The 'herd instinct' describes the same phenomenon. People accept the opinions or follow the actions of others in their group for fear of being seen as outsiders if they take a different course.

Bite 12: Frames of Reference and the Institutionalisation of Theory Formation

Western societies are today run on the basis of a variety of theories relating to the obligations and rights of citizens, what constitutes good conduct, how government should be conducted, how citizens can be maintained in good health, how material wealth can be increased, how it should be distributed, how communal funds should be disbursed and many other issues. These theories are generally the accumulations of decades if not centuries of investigation, transmitted from staff to students in universities, evolving with the circumstances of their times.

In earlier times, societies were run on much more limited theory. A common theory directed the lives of ordinary people and governance was directed by little more. As was seen in Bite 10, common theory has been extended by those who found its explanations unsatisfactory. They were found increasingly unsatisfactory in the context of a growing diversity of human society. They were extended under the influence of the growing acceptance of support conventions that stimulated intellectual support-bargaining. Support for ideas and theories became critical to social ascendancy. The early extensions of common theory in the form of 'natural philosophy', evolving into 'natural scientific' enquiry, proved highly revealing and highly important to social change. Other forms of enquiry of a more 'social scientific' nature were encouraged to follow that lead.

Social theories are influential because they form the 'frames of reference' which cause people to direct their attention to certain phenomena and ignore others, and interpret what they observe in certain ways. Observation and understanding have to fit with the preconceptions provided by these frames of reference. Phenomena that do not fit are likely to be overlooked or ignored. Or when forced upon people's attention, they are likely to be interpreted in such a way as to minimise their significance. In this way, frames of reference assemble support. The support they assemble is readily utilised in political support-bargaining. Politicians of the left will be inclined to see deprivation, poor housing and other social injustices of societies, because such observations are consistent with a socialist frame of reference. They will understand such observations as implying the necessity for redistribution of income and wealth, or legislation against social injustice. Politicians of the right will be inclined to see the prosperity that arises from employment in productive companies and the government service provision made possible by the taxation of companies and the incomes and expenditure they generate.

Given this function of theories, it is clearly desirable for any faction wishing to advance its interests to assemble as much support as it can around a theory that will cause others to share their perceptions and understanding and hence support the factional interest. To assemble majorities in a support-bargaining society, it is necessary to assemble support not just amongst political factions, but in the groups that create the theories by which societies understand themselves. The group support necessary to the establishment of theory means that theories cannot be conceived in impersonal and abstract terms, or purely 'theoretical' terms. They have to be understood as created and sustained by groups through intellectual support-bargaining. 'Theories' exist not as autonomous abstractions but in the minds of the 'theory groups' that create them.

The importance of theory in societies is reflected in the organisation of theory making. Organisation, as was seen in Bite 5, involves focusing the efforts of many individuals to a distinct purpose through the use of hierarchies and money budgets. Organisation introduces incentives to conform to group purposes, or the defined focus of the organisation. 'Institutions' have the same function as organisations, though the term suggests greater permanence and is often associated with the functions of a state. Nation states that adhere strongly to a support convention invariably develop universities and similar institutions for the generation of theory that will assemble support for certain frames of reference, generally expected to be of a truthful and beneficial kind. Such support may then be transferred to factions or parties engaged in political support-bargaining that adopt particular frames of reference. In societies that have only weak regard for a support convention, such institutions are commonly little developed and viewed with suspicion, if not actually suppressed.

While the assumed purpose of academic institutions is normally the pursuit of truth, the organisational arrangements afford scope for the pursuit of non-truth interests (Bite 5). Promotion up the hierarchy, and the increases in income that normally accompany such advance, may be most readily achieved by conforming to the received opinion within an institution. Those that reject the received opinion may be subjected to expressions of withdrawal of support, to the extent that they may find it necessary to move to a different institution. It can be difficult for an academic left of centre to work comfortably in an institution with a 'right wing' culture, and vice versa. There is a 'politics' of theory formation.

The political significance of theories—the ease with which support assembled around a theory can be utilised in political support-bargaining—also distracts academic institutions from the pursuit of truth. Theory makers may opt to reap the rewards on offer for the formulation of theory that assembles support for political factions, rather than that which assembles support for the accurate explanation of social processes.

The institutionalisation of theory making in earlier times led to the emergence of an elite group of theological scholars who exercised considerable authority in their nations. They were the 'experts' in matters that were recognised by everyone as of the utmost importance to the community. The opinions of those outside the institutions were regarded by the insiders as of little significance. They did not have the learning and divine inspiration that were seen as entitling the elite to pronounce on theological issues. Mainstream economic theory has assumed by inheritance something of this elite status. Economists cultivate mysteries of method, including mathematical techniques that are inaccessible to most. Theory is formulated more by reference to texts and authorities than by reference to what is observed and experienced through engagement with economic activities. Those who are not institutional specialists, even though they observe and experience economic activity on a day-to-day basis, are not regarded as having the qualifications necessary to make contributions of any significance. The isolation of academic microeconomists in self-certifying groups in universities has diminished their engagement with the realities of economic affairs to the point where their theories seem irrelevant or even damaging to many outside their community.

The theory of support-bargaining and money-bargaining itself constitutes a frame of reference. Texts written in the context of the theory will select and interpret in accordance with it. It has, however, an important characteristic, in that it directs attention to the function of theories themselves as providing the frames of reference by which people observe and interpret. It provides a 'frame of frames', or a 'theory of theory making'. It explains the fundamental importance of theories to the functioning of societies and the intellectual support-bargaining process by which theories are created and modified. While neoclassical economic theory, and all other theories, offer a single frame of reference, the theory of support-bargaining and money-bargaining suggests the formation of frames of reference as part of the process whereby interests are advanced in a social bargaining system. Adopting the theory of support-bargaining implies a capacity to recognise the understandings derived by people from their membership of different theory groups. Monoframe theories confine their users to particular versions of events. That is what gives them effectiveness as ideologies.

Bite 13: Natural Science and Social Science

The successes of the natural sciences in identifying and quantifying permanent relationships between observed phenomena, mostly of a material nature, have been a major inspiration for the development of social theory. Central to the success of the natural sciences has been the empirical testing of theory. Information provided by theory has to be consistent with information derived from observation. In Britain, the foundation of the Royal Society in 1668 was specifically based on the idea that experiment would advance human knowledge with a degree of security that had not been achieved before. Appeal to authorities would no longer be recognised as determinant. Observations would no longer be interpreted in accordance with the pronouncements of authorities, but would be the foundation of theoretical understanding.

The commitment of early 'natural philosophers' to 'experimental philosophy' implied a commitment to the pursuit of truth about the world, and implicit recognition that speculative philosophy was heavily influenced by the pursuit of non-truth interests. At the time of the foundation of the Royal Society, of course, most Western philosophy retained the assumption of a controlling deity, as described in the Bible. 'Authorities' from church hierarchies, ancient and modern, pronounced on theory and the proper interpretation of observed events. The 'scientific method' that evolved from experimental philosophy can be seen as a means of eliminating as far as possible the influence of non-truth interests on theory accepted into the scientific canon.

It is based on the use of multiple sources to confirm any proposition. If one person conducts an experiment and reaches a certain conclusion, the conclusion may or may not be true. If many people conduct the same experiment and reach the same conclusion, the probability of truth is raised. The principle of replication is fundamental to scientific method. Scientific method requires that experiments and the conditions in which they are conducted are carefully documented so that other scientists can conduct the same experiments in the same or at least very nearly the same conditions. The phenomena that have commonly been the subjects of scientific investigation have generally been of a material nature, or associated with materials, that makes possible repetitive testing of this kind.

Support accumulates for a particular theory if testing produces the consistent results that suggest that it is free from influences relating to the non-truth interests of any particular tester. The idea of support-bargaining nevertheless recognises that experimenters may deploy the same or similar frames of reference, or preconceptions, about certain phenomena. They may then select the same aspects of a phenomenon and interpret them in the same way, whilst missing other aspects of the phenomenon and other possible interpretations. Thomas Kuhn introduced the idea of 'paradigm change' into natural scientific enquiries in 1962. He argued that the paradigms, or frames of reference, employed by natural scientists change in 'scientific revolutions'. These revolutions set natural scientific enquiry off in new directions.

The foundation of the Royal Society can be seen as the re-emergence of common theory, as distinct from 'authority' and theological dogma, as the frame of reference for the conduct of scholarly investigations. The work of the Royal Society received little attention from ordinary people, but it nevertheless investigated phenomena experienced by ordinary people. For perhaps 200 years from the founding of the Royal Society, natural science was conducted on the basis of common theory as frame of reference. Heat, light, materials, space, and time were all conceived by scientists much as in common understanding. Their research refined and quantified the understanding of common theory, but was not incompatible with it. In the nineteenth century, it became increasingly apparent that the natural world was removed from, more complex and less penetrable than its conception in common theory. A universe more vast than had ever been conceived, traversed by electromagnetic waves, was inconsistent with the cosy simplicities of common conception. In the twentieth century, the peculiarities of the natural world became yet more apparent. Common understanding of space and time was displaced by the theory of relativity. The behaviour of fundamental particles called into question common ideas about the nature of matter and causation. Kuhn's theory, perhaps rather belatedly, captured something of the conceptual changes that had been required of natural scientists.

Darwin's theory of evolution by natural selection, published in 1859, marked also notable divergence of natural scientific theory from common theory. It had immediate social impact, since it displaced cherished ideas incorporated in common theory regarding the supernatural origins of humanity. In Britain, common theory can no longer be seen as unquestionably incorporating ideas of divine creation. Most scientists probably work with a common theory as frame of reference that acknowledges natural selection.

Other advances of natural science have had repercussions on society of similar importance. A stream of technological innovations deriving from natural science has made possible continuous successful formatting of companies, enlarging the range of available products and reducing unit costs of production (Bite 16). Most people now look to companies for the incomes necessary to their survival, rather than to landowners. Many of those who do not are employed by governments whose budgets are dependent on the revenues from taxation of the monetary exchanges made by companies.

Social science has evolved with aspirations to the pursuit of truth about human societies in the same way as the natural sciences seek the truth about the natural world. The application of scientific method is, however, impeded by inherent difficulties of replication of phenomena that involve exercise of human volition. Events, behaviour and relationships lack the sameness and stability that is present in the phenomena of the natural sciences. Natural science would be much more problematic if gases, liquids and solids could get up and walk away of their own volition. Nor is it easy to isolate particular social relationships from the general context of human interactions. Social scientists adapt scientific method as best they can to the phenomena they are dealing with, but the limitations inevitably mean that non-truth interests more easily influence the formation of theory. Without the means of regularly establishing high levels of 'probable truth', the way is open for the competitive accumulation of support for theories that advance factional interests. As was seen in Bite 12, there are also positive incentives to the assembly of support for non-truth interests. Much social scientific theory is adapted to the requirements of political support-bargaining.

The economists who created the neoclassical economic model in the late nineteenth century claimed inspiration from physics. Their aspiration was to produce theory that could be reckoned as 'truthful' with a probability comparable to that of physics. Since economic transactions were much concerned with 'things', like the material things of physics, the aspiration seemed promising. It was found necessary, however, to minimise problems of human volition by assuming that humans act with consistent rationality in pursuit of returns defined in terms of income and personal 'utility'. With that assumption, it was possible to construct a mathematical model of the functioning of human monetary exchange. While the mathematics appeared to associate the economic model with physical enquiry, the assumption of human rationality removed it far from physics, since it meant the abandonment of any aspirations to empirical accuracy, and thus the abandonment of what was fundamental to natural science. Neoclassical theory became a mathematical exercise that bore scant relationship to the world of observation and experience. The character of neoclassical economic theory is contrasted with that of money-bargaining in Bite 18.

Notes from the Kitchen

Sources

Bite 10: Common Theory
Chapter 8 of *Support-Bargaining, Economics and Society* (SBES) is on 'Common Theory and Personification'. Chapter 2 has a section on 'Free will and determinism'. The Conclusion ends with a section on 'Determinism and social accountability'. Chapter 10 has a section on 'Symmetry and common theory'. References on free will include: Hodgson (1996, 2004), Wilson (2004/1978), and Max-Planck-Gessellschaft (2008).

Chapter 8 of *Getting It Right* (GIR) has a section on 'Mindset and the emergence of bargaining societies'. 'Mindset' and 'informal theory' in GIR are similar to 'common theory'. Political implications of 'mindsets' are sketched at pp. 183–4. The advance of Sarah Palin in United States politics is discussed briefly in SBES by reference to a 'popular mindset' (p. 78). 'Attitudes' similarly constitute part of 'common theory'. Chapter 5 of *The Evolution of Economies* (TEOE) has a section on 'Attitudes, interests and bargaining positions', dealing with the changes in attitudes that facilitated the industrial revolution in Britain. References on attitudes include: Coleman (1977), Hodgson (2000), Mathias (2001), MacCulloch (2010), Mokyr (2011), North (1990), Rose (2002), and Voth (1998).

Chapter 6 of SBES, 'The Evidence for Support-Bargaining', discusses the link of scientific method to common theory and support-bargaining (esp. pp. 110–13). Sources include: Burnham (1997), Güth et al. (1982), Hoffman et al. (1996), and Sherif (1935).

Reference is made to the creation of common theory through stories in SBES, pp. 161–2. Chapter 5 of *Economics for an Information Age* (EIA) on 'Economics and Behavioural Economics' considers the function of 'narrative' as a frame of reference (pp. 154–5).

For comment on Douglass North's (1990) use of 'bargaining' in the common sense, see the sub-section on 'North's stifled dynamic' in Chapter 4 of TEOE, 'Evolutionary Economics'.

Bite 11: The Support Convention and Intellectual Support-Bargaining
Chapter 10 of *Support-Bargaining: The Mechanics of Democracy Revealed* (SBMDR), 'Intellectual Support-Bargaining', gives an account of theory formation in terms of intellectual support-bargaining.

Intellectual support-bargaining in a civil service is discussed in Chapter 7 of *A Theory of Support and Money Bargaining* (TSMB) (pp. 226–49). Major references include: Heclo and Wildavsky (1974), Wildavsky (1964), Sedgemore (1980), and Crossman (1975).

Chapter 9 of *The Evolution of Economies* (TEOE), 'Information and the Evolution of Communications', discusses the formation of an information interface and the role of information in the industrial revolution in nineteenth-century Britain. References include: Andersen (1996), Backhouse (1993), Hayek 1945, and Hodgson (2001).

The issues broached in Chapter 9 of TEOE are taken up in detail in EIA. The role of media and media theory are discussed in Chapters 7 and 8. References on media include: Innis (1950), McLuhan (1964), Poe (2011), and Davies (2015).

On 'groupthink', see the section of Chapter 6 in TSMB, 'Cohesion and the pursuit of "truth"', drawing on Janis (1972).

On the 'herd instinct', see the sub-section in Chapter 7 of TEOE, 'Confidence and over-confidence'. Morgenson and Rosner (2012) is the main reference for comment on the sub-prime mortgage crisis.

Bite 12: Frames of Reference and the Institutionalisation of Theory Formation

These issues are discussed in Chapter 10 of SBMDR, 'Intellectual Support-Bargaining'; Chapter 11 'Frames and Echoes'; Chapter 12 'Institutionalisation of Theory Making'. The 'frame of reference' or 'paradigm' is widely discussed. SBMRD draws particularly on: Goffman (1986/1974), Mannheim (1960), Kuhn (1970/1962), and Rose (2002). On the exclusiveness of academic thinking, reference is made particularly to Henderson (2001).

The emergence of distinct economic theories as a factor in policy formation is noted in Coleman (1977, pp. 173–4). See also pp. 174–5 in Chapter 6 of TEOE, 'The State and Money-Bargaining'.

On the influence of the 'monastic mode of enquiry' on economic theory making, see the section on 'Development of uncommon theory' in Chapter 8 of SBES.

On Karl Marx's ideas concerning the formation of theory, see TSMB, pp. 194–6; SBMDR, pp. 315–20; SBES, pp. 76–7.

On career pressures, see Chapter 3 of EIA (pp. 88–9), drawing on Earl (1995). On the difficulties of working in a department dominated by an alien ideology, see EIA, Chapter 3 (pp. 89–90), drawing on

Goldman (2003); see also Chapter 4 of SBES, 'Power Elites and Pluralist Democracy' (p. 74), drawing on Bachrach and Baratz (1962).

Bite 13: Natural Science and Social Science
On the particularity of natural scientific phenomena and replication of experiments, see the Introduction to TSMB, pp. 3–7. The discussion of scientific method draws in particular on Kuhn (1970/1962). Reference is made also to: Masterman (1970).

On issues surrounding the foundation of the Royal Society, see the section on 'Development of uncommon theory' in SBES, pp. 168–71. William Beveridge (1937) expresses views regarding the unrealism of neoclassical economics in his farewell address as Director of the London School of Economics, quoted on p. 171 of SBES. In the same context, Beveridge comments on the lack of empirical discipline in economic theory formation—see Chapter 1, 'Information and Interests', in EIA, pp. 16–18.

Spiros Latsis (1976) criticises the lack of concern for empirical evidence in neoclassical economics—see Chapter 4 of EIA, p. 113. The sub-section 'Interpretation of psychological games' in Chapter 6 of SBES, 'The Evidence for Support-Bargaining', discusses the difficulties for neoclassical theory in explaining outcomes of 'ultimatum' and 'dictator' games. The Introduction to TEOE, p. ix, notes that neoclassical theory is based on ideas of equilibrium in economies, when it is plain that economies evolve.

On the formulation of neoclassical theory, see the section on 'Depersonalisation and reason', in SBES, pp. 190–5 drawing on Friedman (1953), Hodgson (1988), and Backhouse (2002).

On economics as ideology, see the section on 'The risks of unrealism' in Chapter 8 of GIR. A further aspect is covered in the section on 'Support-bargaining and Social Darwinism' in Chapter 7 of SBES. Adam Smith's aspiration to show how private interest would be conducive to the public good is discussed in Chapter 4 of EIA, 'Economics and the Information Interface'.

References

Andersen, Esben Sloth, 1996, *Evolutionary Economics: Post-Schumpeterian Contributions*, Pinter.

Bachrach, Peter, and Baratz, Morton S., 1962, 'Two Faces of Power', *American Science Review*, Vol. 56, No. 4, pp. 947–52.

Backhouse, Roger E., 1993, *Economists and the Economy: The Evolution of Economic Ideas*, Transaction.

Backhouse, Roger E., 2002, *The Penguin History of Economics*, Penguin.

Beveridge, William, 1937, 'The Place of the Social Sciences in Human Knowledge', *Politica*, Vol. 2, No. 9, September, pp. 459–79; Farewell Address as Director of the London School of Economics and Political Science, 24 June 1937.

Burnham, Terence, 1997, *Essays on Genetic Evolution and Economics*, Dissertation.com.

Coleman, D. C., 1977, *The Economy of England 1450–1750*, Oxford University Press.

Crossman, Richard, 1975, *The Diaries of a Cabinet Minister, Volume 1: Minister of Housing*, Hamilton/Cape.

Davies, Nick, 2015, *Hack Attack: How the Truth Caught Up with Rupert Murdoch*, Vintage Books.

Earl, Peter, 1995, *Microeconomics for Business and Marketing*, Edward Elgar.

Friedman, Milton, 1953, 'The Methodology of Positive Economics', in Friedman, Milton (Ed.), 1953, *Essays in Positive Economics*, Chicago: University of Chicago Press.

Goffman, Erving, 1986/1974, *Frame Analysis: An Essay on the Organisation of Experience*, Northeastern University. First Published 1974.

Goldman, Alvin I., 2003, *Knowledge in a Social World*, Clarendon Press.

Güth, Werner, Schmittberger, Rolf, and Schwarze, Bernd, 1982, 'An Experimental Analysis of Ultimatum Bargaining', *Journal of Economic Behaviour and Organization*, Vol. 3, pp. 367–88.

Hayek, F. A., 1945, 'The Use of Knowledge in Society', *The American Economic Review*, Vol. 35, No. 4, pp. 519–30.

Heclo, Hugh, and Wildavsky, Aaron, 1974, *The Private Government of Public Money*, Macmillan.

Henderson, David, 2001, *The Changing Fortunes of Economic Liberalism*, Institute of Economic Affairs in Association with Profile Books.

Hodgson, Geoffrey, 1988, *Economics and Institutions*, Polity Press.

Hodgson, Geoffrey, 1996, *Economics and Evolution: Bringing Life Back into Economics*, University of Michigan.

Hodgson, Geoffrey, 2000, *Evolution and Institutions*, Edward Elgar.

Hodgson, Geoffrey, 2001, *How Economics Forgot History: The Problem of Historical Specificity in Social Science*, Routledge.

Hodgson, Geoffrey, 2004, *The Evolution of Institutional Economics: Agency, Structure and Darwinism in American Institutionalism*, Routledge.

Hoffman, Elizabeth, McCabe, Kevin, and Smith, Vernon, 1996, 'Social Distancing and Other-Regarding Behavior in Dictator Games', *American Economic Review*, Vol. 86, No. 3, pp. 653–60.

Innis, Harold, 1950, *Empire and Communications*, Oxford University Press.
Janis, Irving, 1972, *Victims of Groupthink*, Houghton Mifflin.
Kuhn, Thomas S., 1970/1962, *The Structure of Scientific Revolutions*, Chicago. First published 1962.
Lakatos, Imre and Musgrave, Alan (Eds.), 1970, *Criticism and the Growth of Knowledge*, Cambridge University Press.
Latsis, Spiros J., 1976, 'A Research Programme in Economics', in Latsis, Spiros. J. (Ed.), 1976, *Method and Appraisal in Economics*, Cambridge University Press.
MacCulloch, Diarmaid, 2010, *A History of Christianity*, Penguin.
Mannheim, Karl, 1960, *Ideology and Utopia*, Routledge and Kegan Paul. First Published 1936.
Masterman, Margaret, 1970, 'The Nature of a Paradigm', in Lakatos and Musgrave, 1970.
Mathias, Peter, 2001, *The First Industrial Nation: The Economic History of Britain 1700–1914*, Routledge.
Max-Planck-Gessellschaft, 'Decision-Making May Be Surprisingly Unconscious Activity', *Science Daily*, 15 April 2008. http://sciencedaily.com/releases/2008/04/080414145705.htm. Accessed 5 July 2010.
McLuhan, Marshall, 1964, *Understanding Media: The Extensions of Man*, Routledge.
Mokyr, Joel, 2011, *The Enlightened Economy: Britain and the Industrial Revolution 1700–1850*, Penguin.
Morgenson, Gretchen, and Rosner, Joshua, 2012, *Reckless Endangerment*, St. Martin's Griffin.
North, Douglass, 1990, *Institutions, Institutional Change and Economic Performance*, Cambridge University Press.
Poe, Marshall T., 2011, *A History of Communications: Media and Society from the Evolution of Speech to the Internet*, Cambridge University Press.
Rose, Jonathan, 2002, *The Intellectual Life of the British Working Classes*, Yale Nota Bene.
Sedgemore, Brian, 1980, *The Secret Constitution*, Hodder & Stoughton.
Sherif, Muzafer, 1935, 'A Study of Some Social Factors in Perception', *Archives of Sociology*, Vol. 27, No. 187, pp. 23–46.
Spread, Patrick, 1984, *A Theory of Support and Money Bargaining (TSMB)*, Macmillan.
Spread, Patrick, 2004, *Getting It Right: Economics and the Security of Support (GIR)*, Book Guild.
Spread, Patrick, 2008, *Support-Bargaining: The Mechanics of Democracy Revealed (SBMDR)*, Book Guild.
Spread, Patrick, 2013, *Support-Bargaining, Economics and Society: A Social Species (SBES)*, Routledge.

Spread, Patrick, 2016, *The Evolution of Economies: Money-Bargaining, Economic Change and Industrial Revolution (TEOE)*, Routledge.
Voth, H.-J., 1998, 'Time and Work in Eighteenth Century London', *Journal of Economic History*, Vol. 45, pp. 29–58.
Wildavsky, Aaron, 1964, *The Politics of the Budgetary Process*, Little, Brown.
Wilson, Edward O., 2004/1978, *On Human Nature*, Harvard University Press. First Published 1978.

CHAPTER 5

Money-Bargaining

Abstract 'Money' and 'money-bargaining' are creations of support-bargaining. Consumers select by reference to their situation; companies are the specialist money-bargaining agencies of money-bargaining systems. The terms of transactions depend on 'bargaining position', a concept well understood in common parlance, because the dynamic of money-bargaining is close to that of support-bargaining. Mainstream economic theory stresses tendencies to equilibrium and an optimal allocation of resources. It is a mathematical illustration of a philosophical conjecture regarding the propensity of individual interest to promote public interest. Money-bargaining, in contrast, explains economic exchange. Through support-bargaining, ideas of communal interest are established and realised through government budgets. It is one of the great triumphs of money-bargaining that it has made possible the realisation of extensive communal interest.

Keywords Money creation · Money-bargaining · Consumption · Companies · Resource allocation · Communal interest

Bite 14: Creation of Money Through Support-Bargaining

One of the most remarkable outcomes of support-bargaining is 'money', bringing with it the process of 'money-bargaining'. The nature of money means that its use as a bargaining counter makes possible transactions

P. Spread, *A Starter on Support-Bargaining and Money-Bargaining in Twenty-Eight Digestible Bites*,
https://doi.org/10.1007/978-3-030-05231-7_5

that would be difficult or impossible with support as the bargaining counter. The creation of money constitutes a part of the cultural evolution driven by support-bargaining (Bite 2).

The efficacy of 'support' is a matter of psychology—the human need for support and the recognition that support is connected to violence. But being psychological, there is much imprecision and unpredictability about it. People can dissemble about their psychological impulses. They can affirm devotion to a cause whilst actively engineering its failure. They can profess loyalty but act treasonably. There is nothing visible and tangible in support to create a permanent record of its allocation at any particular time. Being a psychological matter means also that support does not come in discernible volumes and cannot be subdivided. It can, however, come in different degrees of intensity. People can support fanatically or with a commitment only just beyond indifference. They can oppose and they can oppose with venom. They can support people rather than ideas. They can support their associates or friends, or those to whom they are obligated, with minimal commitment to the substance of what such people intend to advance. Politics has its shifty and imprecise character because of the nature of support as a bargaining counter.

As was seen in Bite 8, the introduction of formal support-bargaining structures to engage a wide range of people in politics requires the distillation of support to the precise manifestation of a 'vote'. Votes are identifiable and countable, so that 'support' represented as votes can be used in such formal systems. While the support of different individuals is valued differently in informal support-bargaining, having reference to the contribution of each individual to the group, the use of votes puts the same value on the support of all individuals. It thus has both a dispersive and a levelling influence.

Societies can function without money on the basis of support-bargaining. Support holds social groups together. Even when societies are aware of money, they have, in some cases, preferred not to use it, or not to use it for internal bargaining purposes, for fear of disrupting the commitments of support that maintain social cohesion. Many in modern Western societies bemoan an excessive preoccupation with money and its divisive social consequences.

Nevertheless, money provides a precise and divisible bargaining counter that can be used very conveniently as a bargaining counter with precise and divisible goods and services in a money-bargaining system, provided only that the people using it maintain their support for its use.

If a group supports some form of 'money', then it will function as a bargaining counter in the group. Being precise and divisible means that money is countable. Hence, monetary transactions lend themselves to codification in arithmetical terms. People maintain records of their monetary transactions and are able to identify the aggregates of their incomes and expenditures. They form 'budgets' to facilitate control of their expenditures in relation to their incomes when incomes are not received at the same time as expenditures are made.

Group support-bargaining produces support for a remarkable range of ideas and purposes, including the religious beliefs of various groups that seem so fanciful to people of other groups. 'Money' is not difficult to support when its use is so widely beneficial to societies. It plays an essential part in the 'trading' that enables large numbers of people to keep themselves alive. It is the focal concern of companies, the specialist money-bargaining agencies of bargaining societies that have been the driving force behind the great expansion of population and prosperity around the world in the last two hundred years (Bite 16). For all its elusive psychological character, 'support' has capacity to fix firmly in the minds of people such concepts of a society as are universally or near-universally agreed in the society. 'Money' is one of its fixtures.

Being precise and divisible, it has been possible to give money a material form. 'Money' is still generally thought of in terms of coins jingling in a pocket or purse. The perceptual information provided by this material emanation of money helps to sustain recognition of its value. But once the idea of money is well established, it is convenient to use money in the form of paper or plastic, or even just arithmetical codifications on paper or on a screen.

The introduction of money into a community held together by support-bargaining would clearly be disruptive. Instead of receiving support for contributions of goods or services to their neighbours, people would receive money for the same contribution. There would be no quibbling about how much was paid, or how much was contributed, as there could easily be with support. And the assurance of a precise return for a precise contribution would be likely to stimulate efforts to produce and contribute. But still, some societies have feared that the incidence of money would so disrupt support-bargaining that the societies would fall apart. Experience has shown, however, that support-bargaining can be effectively maintained, and societies remain cohesive, even with extensive money-bargaining systems. In fact, the money-bargaining systems permit social provision on a scale that could not be contemplated under a system confined to support-bargaining. The introduction of money, as much as it disrupts support-bargaining in some respects, has made possible the intensification and expansion of support-bargaining (Bites 20, 22).

The disruption to support-bargaining from the introduction of money-bargaining results not simply from the displacement of support by money in transactions. Support-bargaining is a matter of group formation. Group ideas and group sentiment tend to dominate individual inclination. Early societies seem to have been 'conformist', and to have meted out very harsh penalties to those who would not or could not conform. Money-bargaining, however, makes it possible for an individual to flourish independently of the group, or independently of society. An individual successful in money-bargaining can, up to a point, flout the ideas and customs of society, in the knowledge that sufficient numbers will rally to the individual in return for money. The tensions between the individualism of money-bargaining and the group character of support-bargaining lie behind much of the right–left antagonisms of modern societies. Societies that have developed the strongest acceptance of individual entitlements have for the most part been those that gave greatest scope for the use of money and money-bargaining. Those that have most constricted individual entitlement, such as the Soviet Union and the People's Republic of China, have generally offered the least scope for money-bargaining.

Bite 15: Consumer Bargaining Sets

It was seen in Bite 3 that interests are identified by reference to situation. In money-bargaining, this is apparent in consumer selection of products and services by reference to situation. Consumers buy clothes by reference to the size and shape of their bodies. They buy houses that are large enough to accommodate their families. Individual and family budgets form components of situations that impose limitations on what can be bought.

Much of what constitutes 'situation' is 'objective', in the sense that everyone agrees that clothes must be of the right size, and a house will better fit the situation when it is of a size that satisfactorily accommodates the whole family. But the definition of 'situation' is also a matter of judgement. Some will conceive themselves as part of a certain social group that dresses in a formal and modest style, and will choose clothes accordingly. Others will conceive themselves as part of a more cosmopolitan and innovative social group and will choose the sort of clothes that resonate within that group. Both are affected by social support-bargaining. Both men and women have conceptions of their social circumstances, their 'status' in society, the sort of groups they belong to, that impose certain constraints on what they will regard as acceptable clothing. The concepts or definitions of situation to which consumers relate their selections are developed through social support-bargaining. Even the idea of 'satisfactory accommodation' in the size of a house may differ between groups because of different ideas developed through support-bargaining.

The various components of situation each impose certain requirements or constraints on what is selected for purchase. The requirements and constraints will concern not only products and their features, or services and their features, but the potential suppliers. A certain proximity of supplier to buyer may be required, for inspection of goods before purchase, or for delivery after a purchase is made. A supplier for some must be 'reputable'. These requirements and constraints bring about the formation by each consumer of what can be conceived as 'consumer bargaining sets': the sets of products or suppliers that will accommodate the consumer's situation as he or she defines it. With a set established, final selection is a matter of determining 'best fit' to situation. Some products or suppliers may be eliminated as plainly offering features that fit less well to the situation as defined than others. Such a process of elimination may leave just one clear 'best fit'.

Selection may also be conceived as involving modification of the initial definition of situation. Tighter specifications may be imposed, so that fewer products or suppliers fit the modified definition of situation. If products are cheaper than expected, budgetary constraints may be tightened, easing the budgetary constraints on other purchases. Some urgency may be introduced, so that 'immediate delivery' of a product becomes a requirement. With such a tightening process, there is finally only one purchase that meets the revised understanding of situation.

Such a process of consumer selection implies that supplier companies must aim to establish themselves and their products in the bargaining sets of consumers. They will seek to identify the people whose situations are such as to dispose them to deal with the company and buy its products. Given the malleability of situation concepts by reference to social support-bargaining, a company will endeavour to persuade people through dissemination of information that their situation is just that which makes necessary to them the company's products. Much advertising can be interpreted as companies trying to establish their products in the bargaining sets of potential buyers. Much corporate market research is directed at identifying the numbers and locations of people whose situations will evolve in future to require certain products, and certain product features, so that the company can design its products to meet the requirements as 'best fit'. Information accumulated about consumers through social media is valuable because it is information about consumer situations and hence about what consumers are likely to buy.

This understanding of consumer selection contrasts with the ideas of consumer selection in neoclassical economic theory. In traditional neoclassical theory, consumers maximise their utility by buying a product up to the point at which its marginal utility is equal to a 'market price' set through the interaction of aggregate supply and demand for uniform products. Difficulties over the idea of 'utility' have given rise to the suggestion that consumer choice is a matter of preferences between goods, rather than selection of particular goods on the basis of cardinal utility. Even the 'preferences' approach does not, however, entirely eliminate concerns over utility.

Situation-related selection seems an obvious essential to any consumer theory. The idea of marginal utility as the basis of consumer choice has perhaps maintained some support because it has an element of situation-related selection. In the traditional theory, what is already possessed of a particular product dictates the value of additional product. What is already possessed constitutes an element of 'situation'. Hence, it determines further requirements. Someone who already has two loaves of bread is likely to put lesser value on the third than on the first. It will be apparent that the concept of situation-related interest and selection in support-bargaining and money-bargaining is much broader than that of marginal utility theory, involving a much wider and more complex understanding of situation. In particular, it identifies the importance of product differentiation, the provision of different product features, to fit the requirements of different consumer situations. The neoclassical formulation requires uniformity of product.

Bite 16: Companies as Bargaining Agencies

A strong bargaining position requires organisation (Bite 5). In a support-bargaining system, political parties, media organisations and pressure groups constitute the dominant agencies. Companies are the dominant agencies of money-bargaining systems. While people engage in money-bargaining, they are also engaged in social and political support-bargaining. Companies are devoted specifically to money-bargaining. They constitute the specialist money-bargaining agencies of money-bargaining systems.

Companies format to meet a viability condition: revenues must exceed costs. Failure to meet the viability condition over an extended period means a company will not survive. Beyond the viability condition, when revenues are well in excess of costs, companies make high profits and their owners become rich (Bite 19).

The viability condition is simply that: revenues > costs. Revenues are 'sales × price' and costs are 'unit cost of provision × volume of provision'. So the viability condition becomes: 'sales × price > unit cost of provision × volume of provision'. These four variables are interlinked. To meet the condition, the price charged must exceed the unit cost of provision. The price will have an important influence on the volume of sales. The unit cost of provision will commonly depend on the volume of production. Companies set the price of their products by reference to the unit cost of provision, though with allowance also for their assessed bargaining position. A product with rare and attractive features may achieve sales at a price above that which just covers unit cost of provision. Success in meeting the viability condition means maintaining necessary interrelationships between the different components. A level of output has to be adopted that is compatible with a unit cost, and hence a price, that will make possible the necessary level of sales. The skill of business people lies in formatting companies that meet the condition, whether from the outset or after modifications within a manageable time period.

The link between unit cost of provision and the level of provision is often a matter of technology. Technologies may offer low unit costs, but only at high levels of output. A technology is usable in a company format when the unit cost of provision in the volume appropriate to the technology is such that the whole volume can be sold at the price necessary to cover the unit cost. In many cases, different companies can use different technologies to produce similar products at different levels of output and different unit costs, achieving viability because different features of the products attract sufficient sales at the price that covers the unit costs. Thus, furniture can be produced with mass production technology in high volume with low unit costs, attracting large sales at low prices, or it can be 'hand made' in low volume and with high unit costs, with sales to consumers who have the budget capacity to pay higher prices for products with desirable features of quality and design that they see as appropriate to their situations. Many different company formats will often be viable in money-bargaining with goods that share fundamental features of function but also incorporate features that make them especially accommodating to certain consumer situations.

Companies strengthen their bargaining positions by producing new or modified products, with features better aligned to consumer situations, often made possible by technological innovation. The expansion of economies in the industrial revolution of the nineteenth century was largely driven by innovations in technology. The company formats in cotton, iron and railways that drove the industrial revolution arose from technological innovation. The evolution of technologies for use in company formats has played a major role in the subsequent evolution of economies. The ingenuity of people in developing new technologies is thus one major driving force behind economic expansion and advancing prosperity.

Having adopted their format, including selection of technology, and made their investments, companies must generate the revenues necessary to viability. 'Sales' are the one component of the viability condition that is not under the direct control of a company. As indicated in the previous bite, companies have to ensure that their products feature in the bargaining sets of potential buyers. They have to give their products such features as will make clear to potential buyers that they are best suited to their situations. This includes a price, based on the unit cost of provision, that will fit the budget capacity of the necessary number of buyers. Companies disseminate copious information directly and through advertising agencies to ensure that people in situations which will dispose them to buy certain products are persuaded of the virtues of a company's products. Companies spend significantly on advertising, as part of the costs of provision, and with effects on their unit costs, to ensure that their products feature in the appropriate bargaining sets.

Companies have been the essential agencies behind the expansion of economies. They focus the work of many individuals to the particular purpose adopted in their formats. They assemble the inputs, including technology, necessary to the success of their format. The status of companies as independent specialist money-bargaining agencies was recognised in Britain in the legislation of the 1840s permitting limited liability. The limited liability company became a money-bargaining agency owned by individuals whose liability for any losses was limited to their investment. Prior to that, the functions of companies were part of the broader money-bargaining engagements of individuals or groups of individuals. The industrial revolution and the associated evolution of the support-bargaining system marked a transition from a society in which people were mainly dependent on landowners for their livelihoods to a society in which they were mainly dependent on employment with companies. The repeal of the Corn Laws in Britain in 1846 affirmed the emerging dominance of companies and the declining importance of landowners.

This account of companies contrasts sharply with the understanding of companies in mainstream economic theory. In that theory, companies are seen as bringing together resources of land, labour and capital in a production process. All firms in an industry produce precisely the same product and all are so small that they cannot individually influence price. A 'market price' is formed through the relationship between the aggregate output of their uniform product—the 'supply'—and the level of 'demand'. Each company produces up to the point where its marginal cost of production is equal to this 'market price'. If it is objected that business people do not seem to run their companies in accordance with this theory, it is argued that the behaviour of business people has to be interpreted as implying that they act 'as if' they understand the mathematics of marginal cost and revenues. Business people follow neoclassical theory even if they are not aware of it. If it is objected that they could not run their companies in the neoclassical way because their companies are not all small, there is no answer. Companies are not even 'near enough' uniformly small (Bite 13).

Not all mainstream economists have found the 'as if' argument satisfactory. Any theory can be sustained if observations are always interpreted 'as if' they conform to the theory. Neoclassical economists have sought to accommodate the manifest importance of companies with an 'add on' to the neoclassical model. It is argued that companies are formed to minimise 'transaction costs'. The nature of these transaction costs, and their relationship to neoclassical costs, is not well specified. Ronald Coase, the originator of the theory of transaction costs, understood them in part as costs of acquiring information. Use of a price mechanism means incurring costs in assembly of information on prices. But perfect information, the availability of all information necessary to rational decisions on the transactions in question, is an essential assumption of the neoclassical model. The mathematical codification in which the model is formulated requires availability of all requisite information. If information has to be sought, a transaction is automatically removed from the neoclassical context. The model ceases to have application. The 'add on' demonstrates the inadequacy of the model, rather than resolving its problems.

The 'add on' also has its own problems. It is not apparent that company executives direct their efforts specifically at the reduction of transaction costs. If they are doing so, it has to be assumed that they act unconsciously, or 'as if' they were specifically concerned with transaction costs, whatever they may be. They are then acting, in the interpretation of the neoclassical theory group, 'as if' they follow the marginal theory of the model, and by implication 'as if' their companies are very small, and 'as if' they are minimising transaction costs. Common theory, or common observation, suggests that ExxonMobil, General Motors, Apple, Rio Tinto, the corner store, and any other company all do much more than reduce transaction costs. Insofar as they do reduce transaction costs, it is in the context of reducing all costs to meet the viability condition. Neoclassical theory has never been able to comprehend the role and significance of companies.

Bite 17: Bargaining Position

The idea of 'bargaining position' and 'strong' and 'weak' bargaining positions is part of common theory. Everyone knows what such terms mean. It is suggested that we have this instinctive understanding of bargaining position because we learn about it in the course of our earliest experience of socialising, or social support-bargaining. If we have only one or very few people to go to for support, we are in a dependent position, which is a weak bargaining position. If there are many options, we have a strong bargaining position. The sense of bargaining position is easily transferred to the transactions of money-bargaining, since the dynamics of money-bargaining are similar to those of support-bargaining. We can 'bargain' over money transactions because we have learnt to bargain for support.

Yet, the idea of bargaining position has no place in neoclassical economic theory. Exchange is conceived as involving uniform products, with the terms of exchange, the price, determined by aggregate supply and aggregate demand, with the exercise of reason, and all necessary information at hand. Two curves intersect on a diagram to show the 'market price'. There is no unseemly haggling, unscrupulous deception or intrusive enquiry. There is no room for 'bargaining positions'.

In money-bargaining, the terms of exchange are determined by a more complex process. A company, as described in Bite 16, will establish a strong bargaining position by offering products that feature as 'best fit' in the bargaining sets of consumers and other buyers. The more buyers recognise the products as essential, to the exclusion of all other goods from all other sources, the stronger the company's bargaining position. The concept of 'best fit' covers not just the products themselves, but the modes of their provision, including the locations in which they are available. Bargaining position for a company depends on the number of potential buyers in situations, including budgetary situation, that dispose them to acquire the company's products, with the features incorporated in them, and the alternative sources of those same product features, or something close to them. The bargaining position of consumers, as described in Bite 15, and other buyers is determined by the availability of products or sources that feature in their bargaining sets, with allowance for variance of the bargaining sets through reappraisal of situation. Each transaction is unique, though transactions will have common features, and recognition of the common features will influence bargaining positions. The concept of aggregate supply and demand for a product has application only insofar as distinctive features of products and their modes of provision are ignored.

A single supplier of a product having features desired by many people, all with adequate budget capacity, has a strong bargaining position. But the bargaining position changes sharply with the introduction of just one other source. The bargaining position of a single incumbent grocer on a street will be weakened by the opening of a rival grocery on the street. A third grocery store weakens bargaining position still more, but probably not to the same extent as the opening of the first alternative. Bargaining position for a buyer strengthens with the weakening of a company bargaining position. Bargaining position is not simply a matter of sources and features; it depends on information about sources and features. A potentially strong bargaining position may not be realised because of lack of information (Bite 23).

It was seen in the previous bite that companies set their prices by reference primarily to their unit costs, but also by reference to their expected or experienced bargaining position. Companies endeavour to strengthen their bargaining positions by creating uniquely attractive products. Recognising the rare qualities of its product, a company will set a price significantly above the unit cost of the product, instead of using a standard 'mark-up'. If sales disappoint, it will lower its price to something that is less profitable. If a company experiences very high demand for a product, the implication is that it has a strong bargaining position, and it is likely to raise the price to reflect the strong experienced bargaining position. Companies innovate with regard to both products and processes in order to give themselves strong bargaining positions. They seek to provide products that incorporate such features as make them uniquely attractive to potential buyers.

The incumbent grocer in the above example of changing bargaining positions might maintain his bargaining position by buying the new arrival. It has proved difficult to reconcile mergers and acquisitions with the economic model, both technically and ideologically. The basic model conceives many small sellers and many buyers, together determining prices. There have been extensive technical studies extending mainstream economic analysis to cover situations of monopoly and oligopoly, or 'imperfect competition', beginning in the 1930s. The studies generally aim to incorporate monopoly and oligopoly in the neoclassical theoretical framework. But the essential quality of the model, that of producing equilibrium with an optimal allocation of resources, is lost in conditions of monopoly and oligopoly. The recognition that such production arrangements are likely to be detrimental to buyers normally leads to recognition also that government intervention is required to prevent them. Since the major ideological implication of the basic model is that a market free from government intervention is most beneficial to society, the admission of a requirement for government intervention to make the market function as it should undermines a fundamental virtue of the model, as identified in the theory group. The studies of monopoly and oligopoly retain other assumptions of the neoclassical model, regarding, for example, the homogeneity of product and the availability of information. They nevertheless imply partial recognition of bargaining position.

The advantages to be derived from mergers and acquisitions through the elimination of alternative sources of a product are readily apparent through the common understanding of bargaining position. But they also offer opportunities for the reduction of unit costs. They are invariably justified by those proposing them as offering economies of scale. A large volume of output from a company resulting from a merger potentially lowers the unit costs of provision and can consequently result in viability with lower prices to buyers than are possible with a smaller output. Mergers based purely on strengthening of a corporate bargaining position, implying deterioration in terms offered to buyers, will not receive public or political support. Mergers that can be presented as giving rise to a new corporate format with lower unit costs and lower prices are more likely to gain public and political support.

The recognition of bargaining position in common theory has made it politically desirable for governments to prevent the emergence of the very strong bargaining positions that can be built through mergers and acquisitions. Mergers and acquisitions that potentially give rise to excessive control of supply of a product group by one or a few companies require government approval in most countries. In the European Union, each member state administers its competition law in cooperation with others through the European Competition Network. Anti-trust legislation has been prominent in the evolution of the United States economy.

Formal merger or acquisition is not necessary to the coordination of pricing decisions. Companies in competition with one another may find it expedient, with or without explicit collusion, to adopt prices that do not significantly challenge others. 'Price wars' are recognised as potentially disadvantageous to all who engage in them. Business people recognise the advantages of 'orderly markets'. Adam Smith belies his reputation as champion of the efficacy of markets, when he remarks:

> People of the same trade seldom meet together, even for merriment and diversion, but the conversation ends in a conspiracy against the public, or in some contrivance to raise prices.

The requirements of buyers in money-bargaining systems, giving rise to 'demand', are dictated by their situations. This means that concepts of situation adopted by buyers will have an important role in determining their bargaining positions. If the delivery of a new television is urgent to cover some particular event, then options are constrained to those suppliers that can deliver urgently, and to models that are immediately available. The urgency of the situation constrains the bargaining position. A motorist who needs a new door for his car, or a writer who needs a new ink cartridge for her printer, is constrained to certain suppliers who can provide products that fit with the make of car or printer. Their bargaining positions are weakened by their situations.

It was seen in Bite 15 that concepts of situation are influenced by the need of individuals to maintain support in their group or community. This influences individual bargaining positions. A person who determines that ownership of a particular model of car is essential to his social status has a weak bargaining position. It may be reckoned an essential acquisition, yet choice is confined to those dealers who can provide that particular model. Or it may be necessary to have a house in a particular locality, potentially incurring the high costs that arise in a locality of recognised status. Reappraisals of situation change bargaining positions. If an event that requires urgent acquisition of a television can be postponed, or if it can be changed to obviate the necessity for a television, or if a television can be hired for the event, then it may be possible to negotiate more advantageous terms with a dealer for delivery at a later date.

The dependence of bargaining positions on information was referred to above. Buyers and sellers invariably know their own strengths and weaknesses. They may disseminate information that establishes the strength of their own bargaining position. Both will be reluctant to reveal information about weaknesses of their position. A buyer in a hurry to get hold of a television may withhold from the dealer any sense of urgency, for fear that the dealer will take the opportunity to exploit a weak bargaining position. If the dealer thinks that the buyer has plenty of time at his disposal to investigate the options, he may quote a 'special price'. For the most part, in ordinary consumer money-bargaining, buyers and sellers know very little about the situations of the other, and have no obligation to reveal such information about themselves, so routine transactions go ahead at prices set by companies based on general assessments or experience of bargaining position, rather than bargaining positions relating to specific transactions.

'One-off' transactions, or transactions that are large in relation to budget capacity, will commonly merit greater attention to bargaining position and the options available. Information on the situation of the protagonists may materially affect the terms of a transaction. Both sides may think it worth some effort and expense to assemble information on the strengths and weaknesses of the bargaining position of the other, in order to gain the best terms for themselves. Each side will be aware of the necessity of concealing, as far as possible, the elements of their own situation that might suggest weakness of their bargaining position.

The dependence of bargaining position on situation and the malleability of the understanding of situation make bargaining positions fluid. They are not objective, in the sense of established by factors operative independently of human cognition (Bite 28). Their dependence on what people think means frequently that they are heavily dependent on the dissemination and interpretation of information. People can be made to understand that their bargaining position is weaker than they would conceive it if furnished with additional or alternative information. The dependence on information means also that bargaining position can be manipulated by dissemination of false or misleading information. The absence of the concept of 'bargaining position' in neoclassical economic theory has contributed to its general neglect of information issues and poor accounts of information issues where they are addressed. The role of information in support-bargaining and money-bargaining is considered in Bites 23–28.

Bite 18. Money-Bargaining and Mainstream Economic Theory

The mainstream or neoclassical economic theory that dominates academic thinking and teaching was developed in the late nineteenth century by economists from several Western nations, with pride of place generally accorded to the French economist Léon Walras. Prominent contributors included the Austrian economists Karl Menger and Eugene von Böhm-Bawerk, the English economists Stanley Jevons and Alfred Marshall and the American economist John Bates Clark. The theory is termed 'neoclassical' because it derives from 'classical' economics, developed most prominently by Adam Smith, David Ricardo and John Stuart Mill. As might be expected, given the large and varied formulating group, the considerable conceptual difficulties, the varied acceptance of empirical considerations and the extensive supplementary work, there is no single accepted account of the 'neoclassical model'. It is a product of intellectual support-bargaining within academic institutions. It is as varied as the members of the theory group.

The ambiguity might be regarded as a weakness, particularly when the model is claimed to display 'mathematical rigour', but in the context of intellectual support-bargaining, it has made the neoclassical model more defensible than it would otherwise be. It gives the model flexibility and alternatives. Critics find it hard to fix the target. They are dismissed as fixing on a 'straw man'. The knave is never where you last saw it. Nevertheless, two basic characteristics of the model, its portrayal of economic systems as tending to equilibrium and the realisation in the model of an optimal allocation of resources, are unambiguously claimed to justify the use of the model to shape economic policy. 'Optimal allocation' is claimed in the sense that it is not possible to reallocate resources to make one agent better off without making another agent worse off. The use of the model as a frame of reference is justified by reference to such apparent virtues of its application. They are, however, properties only of the most basic mathematical formulation of the model. So if the use of the model is to be justified in terms of those properties, it has to be defended in its basic form.

The basic content can be seen as deriving directly from Adam Smith's concept of 'natural prices'; prices that arise naturally if small businesses compete fully with each other, pushing wages, prices and profits down to the minimum necessary to maintain engagement. The neoclassical model sees something like 'natural prices' being formed through the interactions of many suppliers and many buyers. It codifies in precise mathematical terms Smith's more impressionistic concept of 'natural prices'. 'Supply' and 'demand' for a uniform product become aligned at a 'market price'. Consumer demand is expressed in preferences for the different products coming from suppliers. Consumers continue to buy a product up to the point at which the utility or satisfaction they derive from it is equal to its market price (Bite 15). Companies expand production by buying in resources of land, labour and capital up to the point at which the cost of production is equal to the market price (Bite 16). In both cases, the decisions depend on marginal calculations, so that the model is known also as the 'marginal model'. Adjustments at the margin in response to price changes mean that the system always returns to equilibrium with full employment of resources and their optimal allocation.

Smith's account of 'natural prices' reflects his preoccupation with the relationship between private and public interest. His first book, *The Theory of Moral Sentiments*, investigated the impulses that reconciled human individual interest with the interests of societies. Smith argued that an 'inner man' impelled by reason and sympathy causes people to act in ways that are acceptable in a society. In *The Wealth of Nations*, the concept of 'natural prices' describes a notional state in which prices and profit adjust through competition to keep everyone engaged but to give no one profit beyond that necessity. With natural prices, private interest is conducive to public interest.

Smith's reconciliation of private and public interests through 'natural prices' attracted later economists. In neoclassical theory, 'market prices' fulfil much the same function as natural prices. They give everyone engaged in economic transactions a return commensurate with their contribution, but no more than that. Competition between many small agents, whether producers or labour, ensures that profits are constrained to the minimum required to keep people engaged. There is no scope for profit at the expense of others. Any prices that move out of line are restored to their proper level by the diversion of resources to the relevant activity. Equilibrium is restored, with full employment of resources and optimal allocation. The model is more a mathematical illustration of a conjecture of moral philosophy than an attempt to explain the functioning of economic exchange.

'Natural prices' in Smith's account are not the actual prices experienced in economic transactions. He differentiates between 'natural prices' and 'market prices'. The latter are described by Smith as the actual prices that arise. Fluctuations in supply of commodities and in effective demand cause divergence of 'market prices' from 'natural prices'. He is under no illusions about the realism of 'natural prices'. He excoriates the behaviour of 'merchants and master manufacturers'. They are the agents of the economic sphere that pursue their own advantage with almost total disregard for the interests of society. They 'tax' their fellow citizens by constraining competition so that they can raise their profits. As was seen in Bite 17, they conspire amongst themselves to raise prices. The 'inner man' of such people fails to control their individual avarice, spoiling society and spoiling Smith's conjecture.

Neoclassical economists have frequently opted to overlook these negative elements in Smith's theory, preferring instead to emphasise an 'invisible hand', supposedly the hand of 'the market', that makes their 'market prices' akin to 'natural prices' and brings private interest into accord with public interest. Smith uses the phrase once in *The Wealth of Nations*, in a chapter on foreign trade, with reference to the preference of investors to invest in their own domestic economy rather than overseas. It comes late in his book, well apart from his analysis of domestic markets. But with it, the neoclassical model has been elevated beyond mere exercise in moral philosophy to an explanation, at least 'near enough to be useful', of how economic exchange actually takes place.

The mathematical character of the neoclassical model was presented not as confining but as advancing the study of economics to a status comparable to that of the natural sciences. Through the nineteenth century, physics had been uncovering secrets of the natural world, to the admiration of society. The formulators of the neoclassical model apparently had the potential to shine some of the mathematical light of physics onto the phenomena of economic exchange. But at the same time, their preoccupation with mathematical formulation rendered them insensitive, in varying degrees, to inconsistencies of their theory with information derived from observation. While formulation in mathematical terms took economic theory closer to physical science, the demands of mathematical codification took it far from the empirical discipline that constitutes the bedrock of natural scientific enquiry (Bite 13).

Smith recognised in *The Theory of Moral Sentiments* that an economy functioned in a broader social context, analogous to the way money-bargaining is conceived as taking place in a context of support-bargaining. The analogy is the closer, in that Smith was concerned most fundamentally with the relationship between individual or selfish interest and social or group interest, which is the central dynamic of support-bargaining (Bite 2). In the support-bargaining context, the elevation of the neoclassical model can be seen as related to the rivalry between individual and group interests. A mathematical model that 'proves' individual interest to be advantageous also to the group interest is likely to assemble support amongst those inclined to the individual interest. In the face of surging support for the group interest in the late nineteenth century, the neoclassical model gained sufficient support to establish ascendancy in academic institutions across the Western world.

In Bite 16, the importance of technology in company formats was emphasised. Technology is a major determinant of unit costs, and such costs are linked with the level of output. The very large size of companies today is in large part a consequence of the common feature of most technologies—that unit costs fall as levels of output rise. This applies not just in production but also in distribution, administration, accounting, advertising and other functions of companies. 'Economies of scale' are ubiquitous. One of the major shortcomings of Adam Smith's account of economic processes is the neglect of technology. The arrangements in pin making described at the opening of *The Wealth of Nations* are more the consequence of technology than the division of labour. An industrial revolution based on technological innovation was gathering strength at the time Smith was writing. In pursuing Smith's idea of 'natural prices', neoclassical theory pursued also his preoccupation with the smallest scale of operations, echoed his neglect of technology, and accepted his neglect of economies of scale. The basic neoclassical model, with its tendency to equilibrium and its optimal allocation of resources, cannot accommodate economies of scale. George Richardson has pointed out that if a company gains economies of scale, it is likely to offer prices that smaller firms cannot compete with. It will grow at the expense of others. Thus, in this first and essential step beyond moral and mathematical aspirations into the world of empirical phenomena, the model fails as an explanation of economic exchange and cannot substantiate the virtues claimed for it.

Neoclassical economists sometimes refer to the Arrow-Debreu model as the defining exposition of their theory. It is held to demonstrate conclusively, in a way that the marginal model does not, that free markets will produce the sort of equilibrium that is claimed. The mathematical techniques used are quite different from the calculus of marginal analysis in the standard forms of the model. But the Arrow-Debreu model is similarly unable to accommodate economies of scale. It has been said that this constitutes the major empirical deficiency of the model, though the presumption of the model that all transactions take place instantaneously seems a significant contender for that status. 'Money' has no part in Arrow-Debreu transactions—settlement is by mathematical magic.

The survival of the neoclassical model in spite of its manifest inadequacies is attributed above to support deriving from its justification of individual interest. On this basis, it has provided secure institutional engagement for its adherents. This institutional strength has impeded the emergence of alternatives (cf. Bite 12). The failure to develop alternative theory constitutes a significant factor in the continued ascendancy of the mainstream model. In the understanding of intellectual support-bargaining, theories gain their strength through group support and the confidence engendered by group support. Take away the theory and the group loses confidence. Before theory can change, an alternative source of intellectual support has to be established.

The theory of support-bargaining and money-bargaining provides an alternative based firmly on empirical observation. In spite of the strictures on evidence assembled in the context of support-bargaining, implying uncertainty over even the most apparently well-founded evidence, there is no superior means of establishing the consistency that is the critical factor in determining what is most likely (Bite 13). Neoclassical theory, being a matter of moral philosophy and mathematical rigour, conceives evidence as matter to be interpreted in such a way as to accord with the truths of its model. But problems with evidence go deep, and nowhere deeper than with the evidence that economies evolve. Evolution of economies is consistent with the theory of support-bargaining and money-bargaining, but beyond sympathetic interpretation for a model that cites a tendency to equilibrium as its leading characteristic.

Bite 19: Income Distribution

As was seen in the previous bite, the neoclassical economic model indicates that people are rewarded according to their inputs. Any excessive payments will be rapidly eroded by diversion of resources to take advantage of the high returns available. Incomes become distributed in accordance with an optimal allocation of resources. If incomes are highly skewed, it is a consequence of failure to permit the operation of free markets. Because mainstream economic theory sees no potential for highly skewed income, except as a consequence of ignoring its precepts, the subject has received less attention in economic analysis than is appropriate by reference to common observation or, most notably, a socialist frame of reference.

The specialist money-bargaining agents of a money-bargaining system are companies (Bite 16). They format to meet or exceed a viability condition. Some establish such strong bargaining positions that they spectacularly exceed the viability condition. Large companies are controlled through support-bargaining amongst their boards and senior executives. By this means also payments of dividends and executive remuneration are determined. The owners and executives in charge of highly profitable companies become rich. The owners of small companies can also achieve strong bargaining positions which enable them to exceed handsomely the viability condition. They too become rich. Wealth implies relief from one of the major constraints on the realisation of interests, so it is the ambition of many people to become rich. Business enterprise offers the prospect of realising such ambition.

While many companies fail to meet the viability condition and go out of business, many are able to utilise at least part of their surpluses of revenues over costs to invest and expand. Capacities developed in one area of activity may be extended to a connected area. Common information, research, technologies, human skills and experience, financial specialism, distributional expertise may all provide links between activities which can form the basis of establishment of further viable enterprise. Company formats proven in one activity may be extended to other activities. Money-bargaining positions can be built cumulatively over long periods.

High returns to individual business people arouse adverse reactions amongst advocates of the primacy of the group. Large individual fortunes are reckoned inimical to the well-being of society. The group ideal is equal distribution of income, or something close; certainly not income that is heavily skewed towards a relatively small number of very rich people and away from large numbers of others. Income differentials have widened significantly in the United States and United Kingdom, and some other advanced industrial countries, since 1980. A 'super-rich' one per cent of the top one per cent of the income distribution in the United States has experienced especially high rates of growth in income.

Disparities in individual incomes and wealth reflect more broadly the individualism of money-bargaining, as contrasted with the importance of groups in support-bargaining. As was seen in Bite 14, money-bargaining provides scope for individuals to advance their incomes and influence within a community with little regard for what the community regards as appropriate behaviour. A money-bargaining system strengthens the bargaining position of individuals in a society and strengthens the 'individualist' faction in support-bargaining. The fundamental 'individual-group' tensions of a support-bargaining system, observable in the 'right-left' political divisions in societies, thus come to be associated also with a 'rich–poor' divide.

The mainstream economic model has had the effect of concentrating attention on private individual transactions. A money-bargaining system, however, extends to communal interest as well as individual interest. Support-bargaining brings about the formation of ideas of communal interest (Bites 2, 20), and the establishment of governments through formal support-bargaining makes possible the advance of communal interests through governments. This includes the taxation of private money-bargaining to form government budgets, and expenditures from those budgets on communal interests. Thus, whereas the neoclassical model is purely concerned with private individual incomes and demand, a money-bargaining system is concerned with both individual and communal 'demand'. Analysis of income distribution in a neoclassical economic context tends to concentrate on distribution of private individual income, and ignore the income received 'in kind' by everyone as part of the communal provision through governments.

Thus, a prominent study by Thomas Piketty, published in English in 2014, of income distribution is concerned with individual income and wealth. Piketty is aware of the importance of the 'human capital' that is developed through public expenditure on education and other services but chooses to exclude it from his analysis. It is difficult to codify human capital in arithmetical terms in the way that individual income and wealth are codified, which is probably a further reason for its exclusion. But it makes less than complete sense to establish a system of individual and communal reward and evaluate the system by reference only to individual reward. One of the great communal advantages deriving from the activities of companies described in Bite 16 and immediately above is that their success in money-bargaining makes possible the transfer of large sums in taxation to government budgets from companies and the money flows created by them. The neglect of this communal aspect of income and wealth is the more significant when the conclusion of the analysis is that transfers to government budgets should be increased and education improved.

State expenditures on education and health in particular have substantially changed the people of Western societies. The uneducated and physically ailing are little able to look after themselves. They are largely dependent on others for their livelihoods and can for the most part play only a very minor part in the political support-bargaining that determines the directions taken by their societies. The changes in human capacities arising from the combination of successful money-bargaining and open support-bargaining systems are perhaps the most notable feature of the changes in Western societies over the last two hundred years. As was seen in Bite 16, it is the capacities of the people involved in support-bargaining and money-bargaining systems that determine the levels of technological innovation in a society and hence the growth of money-bargaining systems. Public expenditures on education and health have a much greater impact on the well-being of those in the lower and middle parts of an income distribution than those at the top, who are in a position to provide for themselves.

Piketty's study provides analysis based on the mainstream individualist economic model to demonstrate consequences of the model that will be condemned in a common frame of reference and excoriated in a socialist frame. It thereby assembles support for group-based solutions to the problem, including increased taxation, without regard for the accommodation of group or communal interests, notably the development of human capacities, already accomplished through a system of support-bargaining and money-bargaining. It has to be understood in the context of the process of intellectual support-bargaining described in Bites 10–13.

The theory of support-bargaining and money-bargaining explains a society in which both individual and communal interests are advanced. Companies as the leading agents of money-bargaining, where they successfully meet the viability condition, can achieve high monetary surpluses, so that their owners and senior executives become rich. There is inherent tendency to skewed income distribution in private money-bargaining. But the success of companies increases the revenues available to governments for the advance of communal interests. The advance of communal interests can take many forms, including measures to reduce the inequalities arising from money-bargaining. At a certain point, however, such measures will significantly reduce the transfers governments receive for the provision of communal services. The skew in private income distribution involves also skew in the shares of tax transferred from the different income groups.

Bite 20. Communal Interests and Money-Bargaining

It was seen in the previous bite and in Bite 2 that while the neoclassical economic model can only conceive of individual interests, a support-bargaining and money-bargaining system also involves communal interest formulated through support-bargaining. Governments are the agents of support-bargaining and money-bargaining systems that assume principal responsibility for the realisation of communal interests. Governments engage in money-bargaining through their budgets, though their decisions are dictated by support-bargaining. Neoclassical theory not only confines itself to individual interest, but understands any intervention as likely to be counterproductive—as disruptive of that 'optimal allocation of resources' attendant on the exercise of individual choice in free markets.

As was seen in Bite 16, companies are specialist agencies of money-bargaining systems, responding only to the interests of those with money budgets. Companies characteristically deal with individuals or other companies. Group or communal interests do not command the attention of companies unless a group budget has been established. Groups of many kinds—social, sporting and political—become organised and establish budgets for the advance of the agreed interests of the group. With budgets, they can obtain goods and services from companies. Political groups include, in organised form, political parties, which establish money budgets as an essential part of their efforts to raise the support that will win them seats in a legislature and potentially win them a majority in a legislature (Bite 8). In the 'Westminster system' of formal support-bargaining, a majority in the legislature gives a political party the status of government and control over a national government budget of substantial size in relation to the total money-bargaining of a nation.

Government budgets permit a ruling party or coalition to raise revenues and allocate expenditures in accordance with a communal interest defined through the process that establishes it as government. Through its budget, a government can acquire goods and services from companies and individuals. Governments directly employ large numbers of individuals to perform functions in connection with the delivery of communal services. They compete with companies for the services of individuals in a wide range of skills.

The individual versus group conflict that is fundamental to support-bargaining has led to the formulation of distinct theories 'pro-individual' or 'pro-group', being at the same time 'anti-group' and 'anti-individual' respectively. The theories have been the basis of 'ideological conflict' for generations. But in spite of the conflicts involved, it is readily apparent that the interests of individual and group are in many respects complementary. Neoclassical economic theory sustains its basic tenet that government intervention is detrimental to the working of the private economy; socialist theory maintains that only with extensive communally based industry can the essentials of social justice be delivered. But in the support-bargaining and money-bargaining systems that have emerged in Western democracies and in other countries around the world, it is apparent that companies can only operate with extensive infrastructure and services provided on a communal basis. It is apparent also that with such communal provision, companies are able to expand

and generate private money-bargaining networks from which governments can derive budgetary revenues for the provision of an expanding range of communal services, over and above what is necessary for the functioning of companies. The communal interest is advanced in step with private interest. This constitutes one of the principal means by which private interest enhances the public interest—the original concern behind the formulation of neoclassical economic theory. Yet, this triumph of money-bargaining is beyond the comprehension of neoclassical economic theory. Advocates of group primacy recognise the benefits of government provision as outcomes of their demands for provision in accordance with communal interest and protection, in particular of those disadvantaged by the prominence of companies. But there is also, amongst most, some recognition of the part played by private companies in the provision of individual needs for employment and incomes, and in the provision of revenues to government that permits such copious provision for advance of communal interest. There remains contention over the level and shares of different provision, but the complementarity of individual and group interest in the support-bargaining and money-bargaining systems that have evolved is implicitly acknowledged.

The communal interest identified in the previous bite that enables people to play a full part in the political and economic life of a nation has been a priority in many nations. Education, as was seen, is not just of advantage to the people who receive it, but also, through the innovations that educated people make, of central importance to the evolution of an economy. The acquisition of finance through taxation for communal provision has been less contentious than it might otherwise have been because much communal provision is essential to private money-bargaining, as well as to broader social advantage. People in the ordinary course of their affairs, as well as money-bargaining systems, require laws and regulations regarding the conduct of people towards one another. Both require also the means of enforcement. Constraints on the provision of false information are advantageous to those engaged in money-bargaining and in the general conduct of human affairs. People shy away from systems which cannot be depended on to provide what is reasonably expected and contracted.

Transport infrastructure, such as roads and railways, has both communal and commercial importance. It provides social amenity. It extends the reach of companies, enabling them to feature in the bargaining sets of distant buyers (Bite 16), and hence makes it easier to meet the viability condition. It has been widely agreed as a matter of communal interest that governments should provide extensive transport infrastructure. Transport services themselves, such as trains and buses, are often also provided by governments as matters of communal interest.

The specialisation of companies in money-bargaining entails some insensitivity in them to the wider consequences of their activities. Communal interest has been recognised in protection against some of these consequences. Noise and air pollution are common side effects of the operations of companies that impinge on communities. 'Smoking chimneys' provided the central example of the 'externalities' identified by economists in their efforts to reconcile the basic model with a broader understanding of social advantage. Global warming, environmental damage and extinction of species are all issues that have been defined and brought to international attention through communal support-bargaining in recent decades as consequences of the activities of companies. Extensive regulations have been introduced to protect the communal interest.

Communal interest has been identified also in the provision of money or benefits in kind by governments to poor people or people otherwise in adverse circumstances. This constitutes in part support for the transfer to governments of recognised individual moral obligations to charitable support of the disadvantaged. As money-bargaining systems expand, the more it is possible to allocate funds to support of the disadvantaged.

The government budgets that are central to the advance of communal interests have their own distinctive impact on the assembly and loss of support. Increases in expenditures generally increase support for a government, while higher taxation tends to reduce support. Cash going into people's pockets gets support from the beneficiaries, while cash taken out of people's pockets loses the support of the deprived. There is consequently a natural tendency of governments to spend without raising taxes, and cover the difference with credit.

Debt servicing necessarily displaces expenditures on matters of communal interest, so that the use of credit can be to a large extent pursuit of current communal interest at the expense of future communal interest. 'Self-liquidating' debt, involving money expended for purposes that themselves produce the revenues necessary to service the debt, is easily advocated, but the money is also easily diverted to purposes that return more immediate support. The control of budgets through support-bargaining means that there is constant potential for build-up of debt beyond a level that can be serviced without uncomfortable constriction of expenditures relating to other communal interests.

Bite 21: Microeconomics and Macroeconomics

The depression of the 1930s caused concern amongst neoclassical economists. The theory group had come to believe that its mathematical model did actually explain how economies functioned, so it was puzzled to find that economies across the Western world were not returning to equilibrium with full employment of resources. The credibility of the profession was at stake.

Earlier reaction to unemployment had centred on the study of business cycles. In the United States, President Herbert Hoover, following his own recommendations as chairman of the President's Conference on Unemployment in 1921, undertook counter-cyclical public expenditures in response to the Wall Street Crash of 1929, though the programme was not sustained. In Sweden, counter-cyclical public investment was made in accordance with home-grown theory. In Britain, John Maynard Keynes, whose father John Neville Keynes, was also a prominent economist, came up with a modification to neoclassical theory that purported to explain the shortfall in employment. *The General Theory of Employment, Interest and Money*, published in 1936, identified the root of the problem as 'demand deficiency' and 'involuntary unemployment'. Since private business seemed ill-suited to undertake the investment that would offset 'demand deficiency', Keynes concluded that a 'socialisation' of investment was necessary to ensure full employment.

William Beveridge (who later prepared the 'Beveridge Report' that formed the basis for the United Kingdom National Health Service) pointed out shortly after publication that Keynes concentrated on theory rather than on facts or observation. Keynes starts with a definition of 'involuntary unemployment' and continues with a series of other definitions, all of which conduct the student inexorably to the conclusions that Keynes wanted to arrive at. The definitions arise from theoretical understanding; their relationship to observed phenomena is open to question. Amongst Keynes's further definitions is savings as 'the excess of income over consumption'. Keynes's theory has been greatly venerated. It has been seen as part of a 'neoclassical synthesis'—aligning the microeconomic neoclassical model with macroeconomic processes.

Keynes's definition of 'involuntary unemployment', the subject of Beveridge's comment, is immediately problematic:

> Men are involuntarily unemployed if, in the event of a small rise in the price of wage-goods relatively to the money-wage, both the aggregate supply of labour willing to work for the current money-wage and the aggregate demand for it at that wage would be greater than the existing volume of employment.

Academic enquiry emphasises the importance of definition as a means of clarification and a means of forestalling later semantic debate over 'meaning'. Keynes's definition of involuntary unemployment does not seem to fit this role. It seems to relate to a hypothetical situation. There seems no way in which involuntary unemployment could be empirically confirmed.

But definition has a second function, much less evident in academic debate. Definitions are necessarily made by reference to a particular frame of reference, and are specific to that frame of reference. By accepting definitions, respondents become locked into a particular frame of reference, and are more likely to assent to whatever analysis follows. Keynes's definition of involuntary unemployment seems to conform to this understanding of definition. It moves debate out of the neoclassical frame of reference, in which the labour wage would reduce so that supply matched demand, and into a Keynesian frame of reference. It seems then that people can remain unemployed in low-level equilibrium whether or not they are prepared to agree on a wage with an employer.

A second definition, equally critical to Keynes's scheme, is that of 'savings'. The essential innovation of Keynes's account of the functioning of an economy lies in the determination of savings through an 'income effect' rather than directly through changes in interest rates, as in the neoclassical model. Keynes's definition of 'savings' as the residual of income after consumption expenditure makes possible the 'income effect'. Savings can equate to investment at incomes below those necessary to ensure full utilisation of resources, and in particular without full employment. 'Savings', like unemployment, become involuntary. They depend on incomes and consumption rather than interest rates.

Keynes recognises several reasons to save, or as he terms it, 'refrain from consumption'. In money-bargaining, the impulse to save relates, as all other interests, to situation. People recognise in their circumstances that requirements will arise for funds for holidays, emergencies, family events, old age and other purposes. 'Saving' is purposeful and much of it will have priority over consumption. If there is 'residual money', it is money remaining as a budget surplus after consumption and savings allocations. The lack of any proper concept of time in the neoclassical model means that there is no place for the concept of a 'budget' by which disparities in the time of receipt of income and the making of expenditures are accommodated. There is then no concept of budget surplus or deficit, or of unallocated funds.

Keynes's definition has perhaps been acceptable because there is a colloquial sense in which what is not spent is 'saved'. If you refrain from buying a bag of crisps, you have 'saved' that money. But 'save' is also used in a colloquial sense when advertisers insist that 'the more you spend the more you save', with reference to discount sales. 'Saving' in money-bargaining has distinctive situation-related purpose and often high priority. It is then conceptually misleading to make no distinction between 'saving' and budget surpluses or deficits. With Keynes, the more colloquial sense becomes the foundation for major theoretical construction and policy recommendations.

In the understanding of money-bargaining, the assessment of savings requirements by reference to situation and the assessment of investment requirements by reference to the evolution of company formats means there is no reason to anticipate alignment of savings with investment. The different assessments nevertheless provide opportunities for the format of companies to lend available funds to those who have need of them. Financial services companies meet the viability condition by raising revenues in the form of interest payments from borrowers whilst paying interest on funds made available by savers and depositors. Finance on varied terms is provided to fit the circumstances of borrowers, whilst many different options, aligned to their various situations, are offered to attract the funds of savers and depositors. Financial services companies have often handsomely exceeded the viability condition.

In the understanding of intellectual support-bargaining, frames of reference are formulated to direct observation and interpretation in ways favourable to the interests of the formulators (Bite 12). It is the way theories are created. Keynesian economics illustrates the process. Keynes provides definitions on the basis of certain preconceptions, which are in effect the conclusions he wishes to arrive at. The definitions create a frame of reference in which his desired theoretical outcomes are apparently realised. Beveridge points out their lack of empirical consistency. All theories are frames of reference which involve this circularity of perception and interpretation. Keynes uses it to assemble support for a modified form of neoclassical theory. It provided a lifeline for neoclassical economists.

Keynes's macroeconomy is all but devoid of technology. Keynes's economic transactions take place 'in a given state of technique'. The evolution of technology is an important part of the evolution of companies and the evolution of an economy. Technological change is an important factor in the loss and creation of employment, so that something important is missing from a 'general theory of employment' that does not take account of technological factors. Keynes and most of his readers tolerate such omission because the neoclassical context is similarly devoid of technological considerations. In this instance, Keynes's macroeconomy is compatible with the microeconomics; they make the same omission. But, of course, a real macroeconomy evolves with the evolution of technology, and the neoclassical model has neither technology nor evolution.

The omission of technological considerations gives Keynes's 'investment' a homogeneity that is inappropriate. 'Investment', for Keynes is just 'the current addition to the value of the capital equipment which has resulted from the activity of the period'. 'Investment' is defined as the difference between output and consumption, while saving is defined as the residual of income after consumption, so that investment is equal to saving. Keynes's recommendation for 'socialisation' of investment suggests that the necessary units of investment can be installed by anyone. It is just a matter of aligning investment mathematically with savings at the level necessary to full employment. He argues that state officials will be better able to 'calculate the marginal efficiency of capital goods on long views' than private investors. But state officials will not know the latest technology in the many sectors and sub-sectors of an economy, and its implications for company formats. Innovative companies with innovative technologies are required to make investment effective in the beneficial evolution of economies. Keynes seems unaware of historical accounts of the activities of large companies. Alfred Chandler's later accounts of the role of large companies in economic development make plain their significance.

Keynes's theory, like neoclassical microeconomics, is a mathematical theory. While neoclassical microeconomics is concerned with a conjecture of moral philosophy, Keynes's theory constructs a mathematical escape from the difficulties of unemployment. In economic terms, unemployment is important in the context of 'full use of resources', but 'unused land' does not attract the same attention. Unemployment is important because people suffer when unemployed and as a consequence of that governments lose support over unemployment. Full employment is a communal interest. For those steeped in neoclassical style and content, Keynes's theory was plausible, but only because it sustained the basic misconceptions of neoclassical theory. Keynes restored the confidence of the mainstream economic theory group, but at great cost to the understanding of economic processes.

The neoclassical model is concerned with purely private and individual transactions, whereas macroeconomic processes involve governments as agents of communal interest. A significant part of 'income' is neither consumed nor in any sense 'saved', but is compulsorily transferred to governments for the accommodation of communal interests. The state plays no part in Keynes's conception of an economy except as a rescue service when private investors fail to achieve required levels of investment. There is no such thing as 'communal interest'. Keynes's theory is just one amongst the many extensions and supplements to the neoclassical model that seek to interpret observable realities in a way that renders them compatible with the model, though all they do is demonstrate that it is untenable.

Money-bargaining is both microeconomic theory and macroeconomic theory. The 'macroeconomy' is the sum of the budgets of all the agents, including central and local government, that engage in money-bargaining. The linkage between budgets means that disruptions to one budget are transmitted to others. The larger the budget that is disrupted, the larger the potential disruption to others. The theory of money-bargaining is largely compatible with the macroeconomic theory implicit in national income accounts. These accounts were developed in their modern form mainly in the early 1940s, responding to a pressing need to identify resources available to governments for the conduct of the war against Nazism. While they retain the neoclassical concept of resource allocation, they were drawn up with very pragmatic purpose, so that theoretical preconceptions were not permitted to inhibit realistic assessment of economies. The importance of time, geography, governments, innovation and information, and the irrelevance of equilibrium, required the marginalisation of marginal theory. That empirical priority links national accounts to money-bargaining. The incompatibility of mainstream microeconomic theory with macroeconomic theory has been a continued source of embarrassment to mainstream economists. The application of microeconomic principles to macroeconomic circumstances was part of the mishandling of the financial crisis that exploded in 2008. The macroeconomic research based on the neoclassical microeconomic idea of equilibrium has been notably unfruitful.

Bite 22: Linkages of Support-Bargaining and Money-Bargaining

People act to gain support from their associates. They also act to gain money. To get action, therefore, there may be a choice between support-bargaining and money-bargaining, or they may be used in conjunction, so as to reinforce one another, or one may be used to thwart transactions of the other. People will be inclined to select whichever, or the combination, that best advances their interests.

The creation of money by support-bargaining set up the choice. As was seen in Bite 14, money and money-bargaining are best understood as created to provide a supplementary or alternative system of exchange to support-bargaining. Money-bargaining is the cultural offspring of support-bargaining. Support-bargaining and money-bargaining have a similar dynamic, so that people bring to money-bargaining the sort of haggling skills they know from support-bargaining. The differences arise from the qualities of the bargaining counters 'support' and 'money'. 'Support' is a matter of psychological concern for all individuals, making it the basis of group formation. Money is precise and a matter of individual interest (Bite 14). This difference means that they can be used in a complementary fashion, or the qualities of one counter can be used to counteract the attractions of the other.

'Support' generally has greater significance in a social bargaining system than money because of its associations with violent capacity and its role in the furtherance of group interests. But ruling through successful assembly of support invariably involves also the supplementary incentives of money. Political parties raise budgetary revenues and disburse for the assembly of support. Donations to political parties can be seen as expressions of support in monetary form. Group interest derived from support-bargaining supplemented by individual interest based on monetary incentives concerts action to give a cause strong impetus. Governments use budgetary provision to consolidate their support.

In March 2015, the British Chancellor of the Exchequer introduced a savings scheme for pensioners with interest rates significantly above market rates. Older people are more inclined to vote Conservative than the young, and the scheme was seen by commentators as a means of ensuring that pensioners turned out to vote Conservative in the general election in May of that year.

Support-bargaining and money-bargaining interlock closely in the fulfilment of communal interests through government budgets, as described in Bite 20. Communal interests are identified through support-bargaining but to a great extent realised through money-bargaining. Support-bargaining determines the taxes that can be raised for communal purposes. Even private consumer interests are in part shaped by support-bargaining. It was seen in Bite 15 that what consumers buy is influenced by the concepts of situation they form through social support-bargaining.

The primacy of support and support-bargaining means that support-bargaining can be used to override considerations of money-bargaining. A money-bargaining system is regulated through support-bargaining, but support-bargaining can also be used for more specific interventions to ensure that money-bargaining functions in a way acceptable to ascendant agents of support-bargaining. It was seen in Bite 17 that governments have intervened extensively in relation to mergers and takeovers. Planning regulations are widely applied to determine the location of private business. More specific and contentious interventions, some covert, may determine the behaviour of money-bargaining agencies. Beyond support-bargaining, 'protection rackets' threaten violence to money-bargaining agencies that do not conform to the demands of organised crime. Some governments are little more than organised crime syndicates.

While money-bargaining is used to supplement the pursuit of support, such use implies also some cession of the purity of support-bargaining. Those who provide money to political parties influence the policies of the parties. This and the recognition of money-bargaining agencies that their transactions are subject to 'political' intervention makes agents of both systems feel that they need protection against the other. People generally come to conceive certain areas of activity as 'political matters', or matters of support-bargaining, while others are matters of 'business', or money-bargaining. Transgression of the boundaries is regarded as 'unethical'. It is an expression of the individual-group contention that is the basis of support-bargaining.

The conception is given further expression in the theories developed for the conduct of societies. 'Democracy' is concerned with the conduct of matters pertaining to government, while 'neoclassical economic theory' is concerned with the independent conduct of monetary transactions. The theories are of an idealistic type, implying a universal interest in independent and unsullied operation. Democratic principles require that the will of the people be exercised without any intrusion of financial considerations. Neoclassical economic theory implies that individuals should be free to conduct monetary transactions in 'free markets' unconstrained by political intervention.

The linkages between support-bargaining and money-bargaining are integral to the functioning of Western systems of government. The two systems are heavily interdependent. The insistence on independent theories has led to misunderstanding of the essentials of social bargaining societies, particularly with regard to the role of money-bargaining (Bite 18). Both Piketty (Bite 19) and Keynes (Bite 21) analyse macroeconomies as if government had no part, and then recommend that government steps in to remedy the defects.

Money given to political parties supplements their efforts to assemble support, with an inevitable influence on party policies. Money can be used not just to influence but actually to thwart the determinations of support-bargaining. The individualism of money means that individuals can be diverted from group obligations by money. Those employed by government for the advance of group interests may see their individual advantage in acceptance of private money payments for the moulding of government service in accordance with the private interests. A planning application may be approved in exchange for a private money payment rather than rejected in accordance with regulations established through support-bargaining. A government contract may go to a company that makes a monetary payment to an influential official. Legislation against such practices attaches risk and potential retribution to them and hence diminishes their incidence. Even so, the precise and individualistic character of money, and the ease with which such transactions can be hidden, mean that it can easily be used to divert benefits properly allocated through support-bargaining for the advantage of individuals who pay.

The media castigate the use of budgetary measures to raise support, such as the savings arrangements for pensioners, as 'bribery of voters'—they advance narrow interests through payments of money to the detriment of broader interest pursued through support-bargaining. The media themselves, however, are integrally caught up in the interlinking of support-bargaining and money-bargaining. It was seen in Bite 11 that the media are for the most part companies whose continued existence depends on their meeting the monetary viability condition. Yet, at the same time, they pursue political purposes. The arrangement whereby money-bargaining agencies have the main responsibility for dissemination of information that is a primary influence in the distribution of support in a society appears to be highly unethical, given the ethical understanding set out above. The role of the media is considered further in Bite 27.

Existing social theory is conceived as identifying some singular truth relating to the conduct of government or economic transactions. Democratic theory and economic theory imply different kinds of people, the first devoted to the 'general good' and the latter self-interested. It is then difficult to recognise and understand the mixing of such singular truths and such different people. But while such theories are ostensibly expressions of singular truth, they are easily seen as outcomes of intellectual support-bargaining for the advance of particular interests. They express principles by which it is desired societies should be conducted, rather than how they can actually be observed to function.

Notes from the Kitchen

Sources

Bite 14: Creation of Money Through Support-Bargaining

Chapter 2 of *A Theory of Support and Money Bargaining* (TSMB), 'Support as a Bargaining Benefit', introduces the idea of 'support' as a bargaining counter and contrasts it with the function of money. The chapter draws on: Hicks (1967), Wildavsky (1964), Lindblom (1959), Thibaut and Kelly (1959), Dahrendorf (1959), Coser (1956), and Blau (1964).

Chapter 6 of *Getting It Right* (GIR), 'Links Between Money-Bargaining and Support-Bargaining', describes the differences and similarities in the use of the two bargaining counters. 'Money' is contrasted with 'support' as a bargaining counter (p. 135). Further comparison of money-bargaining and support-bargaining is made at pp. 185–6.

Public choice theory treats politics by reference to neoclassical economic theory, with 'votes' as the countable political counterpart of money. In Chapter 2 of TSMB, a section 'Politics as economics' assesses public choice theory by reference to support-bargaining. References include: Schumpeter (1954), Mueller (1976), Downs (1957), Arrow (1963), Buchanan and Tullock (1965), and Hotelling (1929).

Public choice theory is also referred to in Chapter 2 of *The Evolution of Economies* (TEOE) in the section 'Support-Bargaining and the Impossibility Theorem'. This responds to Arrow (1950).

The nature of money is described in Chapter 9 of *Support-Bargaining, Economics and Society* (SBES), 'Money-Bargaining and the Evolution of Economies', with reference to William Mariner's account of first encounters with money in Tonga, as recorded in Martin (1991/1817).

The same chapter (p. 204) notes Peter Kropotkin's (2003/1902) description of communities that shun the use of money. Chapter 9 also notes the implications for individual advantage of the introduction of money (pp. 204–6). Individualistic qualities of money are described in Chapter 2 of TSMB (pp. 18–19).

The nature of money is also described in Chapter 2 of TEOE, 'Money and Money-Bargaining', This chapter traces (pp. 15–19) the evolution of money as a matter of cultural evolution. It draws on Kropotkin (2003/1902) and on: Menger (1892) and Davies (1994).

Bite 15: Consumer Bargaining Sets

The idea of situation-related selection is set out in Spread (2011). Sources include: Bruni and Sugden (2007), Earl (1986), Hodgson (1988), Jenner (1966), Lancaster (1966), Latsis (1976), Maslow (1970/1954), Sen (1984), Stigler (1961), and Veblen (1994/1899). Hands (2010) provides an account of the historical development of consumer theory.

Chapter 1 of GIR, 'Reality and the Economic Model', provides a summary account of the economic model and analyses the difficulties over marginal utility. It describes 'situation', bargaining sets and bargaining position. Chapter 2 questions marginal theory in the context of the 'Jade-Bread Paradox' (pp. 42–5). Sources include Baumol (1999), Jenner (1966), Lancaster (1966), Earl (1995), Akerlof (1970), Stigler (1961), Bain (1954), Lamberton (1971), and March and Simon (1993/1958).

Chapter 3 of TSMB, 'Bargaining Sets and Bargaining Position' has an account of these aspects of money-bargaining. The section 'Bargaining sets and bargaining position' covers consumer choice. The chapter uses selected anomalies of neoclassical theory to show the superior explanatory capacities of money-bargaining. The anomalies are those identified in Jenner (1966) regarding product differentiation, Stigler (1961) regarding information, Akerlof (1970) regarding quality and Bain (1954) regarding barriers to market entry. Other sources include those listed under GIR above and Weber (1949) and Kuhn (1970/1962).

Chapter 3 of *Support-Bargaining: The Mechanics of Democracy Revealed* (SBMDR), 'Money-Bargaining: Situation and Sets', provides further analysis. This draws additionally on Earl (2004).

Bite 16: Companies as Bargaining Agencies

On the nature of companies, see Spread (2016b). References include: Coase (1937), Cyert and March (1963), March and Simon (1993/1958), Simon (1997/1947), and Williamson (1975). Coase's theory of transaction costs is discussed in the article (esp. pp. 732–4), and also in the section 'Coase and transaction costs' in Chapter 4 of TEOE, and further at pp. 167–8. On the nature of companies, see also TEOE, Chapter 2, 'Money and Money-Bargaining', pp. 29–33, and SBES, pp. 18, 206–8.

Chapter 5 of TEOE. 'The Evolution of Money-Bargaining' describes the company formats that formed the basis of the industrial revolution in

Britain. Sources include: Coleman (1977), Mathias (2001), Deane and Cole (1962), Crafts (1986), Wrigley and Schofield (1981), Thompson (1991), North (1981), Hodgson (1988, 2000), Mokyr (2011), Rose (2002), Micklethwait and Wooldridge (2005), Wrigley (2010), Ashton (1968/1948), and Chandler (2005).

The 'as if' argument originated with Milton Friedman (1953). For comment, see SBES, pp. 192–3.

Bite 17: Bargaining Position

TSMB Chapter 3 is on 'Bargaining Sets and Bargaining Position'. Main sources are recorded under Bite 15.

A section on 'Bargaining position' in Chapter 3 of SBMDR gives an account of the subject. Bargaining concepts get little attention in mainstream economics. Douglass North makes frequent references to 'bargaining' and 'bargaining position' in North (1990). The sub-section 'North's stifled dynamic' in TEOE comments on his usage.

The innovative works on monopoly and oligopoly were Robinson (1979/1933) and Chamberlin (1962/1933).

Quotation is from Smith (2009/1776, p. 99).

Investigations to ascertain bargaining position are described in Spread (2015a).

The importance of information to bargaining positions means that sources provided in Bites 23, 24, 26 are also relevant here. *Economics for an Information Age* (EIA) explains the importance of information.

Bite 18: Money-Bargaining and Mainstream Economic Theory

The origins and essential features of neoclassical theory are described in GIR, Chapter 1, 'Reality and the Economic Model', and in Chapter 2, 'Situation and Sets'. The reference works of the writers mentioned are: Smith (2009/1776), Ricardo (2010/1817), Mill (1884/1848), Walras (2003/1874), Menger (1950/1871), Jevons (2013/1871), Böhm-Bawerk (1959/1884–1912), Marshall (1920/1890), and Clark (1925/1899). Other sources are those shown for GIR Chapters 1 and 2 under Bite 15.

Adam Smith explains natural prices and market prices in Smith (2009/1776), Book 1, Chapter 7: 'Of the Natural and Market Price of Commodities'. His comments on merchants and master manufacturers are at pp. 51, 190–1. Smith refers to the 'invisible hand' in Book 4, Chapter 2: 'Of Restraints upon Importation from Foreign Countries of

Such Goods As Can Be Produced At Home' (p. 325). Smith's book on moral philosophy is Smith (1976/1759).

The derivation of neoclassical theory from Smith's idea of natural prices is described in Chapter 4 of EIA, 'Money-Bargaining and the Information Interface'. Sources include Heilbroner (2017), Hennings (1986), Backhouse (2002), and Robbins (1932). See also SBES, pp. 170–1 and references under Bite 13.

Milton Friedman (1953) is amongst those using the 'near enough to be useful' argument. Heilbroner (2017), Akerlof and Shiller (2015) (p. 5), amongst many (including the present author in earlier work—see SBMDR, pp. 289, 424–6), portray the 'invisible hand' as the hand of the market. For non-specialist writers on economics, whether for or against 'markets', the 'invisible hand' is an irresistible metaphor.

On economies of scale, see SBMDR, pp. 107–9, 261–3; TEOE, pp. 51–4, 296. On Smith's neglect of technology, see SBMDR, pp. 424–5. The main source is Heilbroner (1999).

George Richardson (1990/1960, p. 31) pointed out that economies of scale are incompatible with the neoclassical model. See also EIA Chapter 4, 'Economics and the Information Interface', p. 130.

The section 'The Arrow-Debreu Model', in Chapter 3 of TEOE, pp. 49–55, discusses the Arrow-Debreu model, drawing most particularly on Geanakoplos (2004).

Bite 19: Income Distribution

Thomas Piketty's book is Piketty (2014). Deirdre McCloskey (2014, pp. 88–9) criticises Piketty's omission of human capital.

On human capacities, see the section on 'Communal interest and government' in EIA, Chapter 4.

Bite 20 Communal Interests and Money-Bargaining

The section 'Communal interest and government' in Chapter 4 of EIA explains the role of government, drawing on Searle (1996), Smith (2009/1776). The section emphasises the importance of human capacity.

Chapter 7 of TEOE, 'Support-Bargaining, Credit and Confidence', discusses government budgeting and theories concerning government use of credit. Sources include: Keynes (1961/1936), Backhouse (1993), Mathias (2001), Thornton (1802), Mokyr (2011), and Morgenson and Rosner (2012).

Arthur Pigou (1932, 1933) investigated the wider social welfare implications of the activities of private companies, including the problem of 'smoking chimneys'. The subsections in Chapter 4 of TEOE, 'Social costs and transaction costs', and 'Coase and social bargaining theory', consider the issues, with special reference to Coase (1960).

Chapter 6 of SBMDR, 'State Provision and Private Format' considers issues relating to state modes of provision for communal interest and private format.

The section 'Attitudes, interests and bargaining positions' in Chapter 5 of TEOE describes the changes in attitudes and education that were part of the industrial revolution in Britain. The section 'Railways and companies' in the same chapter describes the importance of the formatting of railway companies for provision of transport infrastructure and services, and the important role of the state in facilitating land acquisition.

Part 5 of Chapter 13 of SBMDR, 'Financial Requirements for a Bargaining Society', traces the historical cooperation and conflict in Britain over state and private engagement in money-bargaining.

Bite 21: Microeconomics and Macroeconomics

The section 'Keynes versus money-bargaining' in Chapter 7 of TEOE provides a detailed discussion of Keynes (1961/1936). Keynes's definition of 'involuntary unemployment' is on p. 15, with original italic emphasis. Sources include: Backhouse (1993, 2002), Chandler (1977, 1990, 2005), and McLeay et al. (2014a, b). A section 'Employment, borrowing and business cycles' in Chapter 7 of TEOE is concerned with business cycles.

Quotations from and references to Keynes's (1961/1936) *General Theory*: defining savings and investment, p. 62; reasons to save, pp. 107–8; recommendation for 'socialisation' of investment, p. 378; reference to 'a given state of technique', p. 23, with similar references at pp. 24, 28, 245; definition of investment, p. 62; marginal efficiency of capital, p. 164.

On the functions of 'definition', see the section 'Institutions, players and definitions' in Chapter 4 of TEOE, and pp. 179–81, 224–5, 242–3. Sources include: Hodgson (1997), Hodgson (2006), North (1990), Marshall (1920/1890), and Robbins (1932).

Chapter 3 of TEOE, 'Macroeconomics and Money-Bargaining', especially the section 'Microeconomics and macroeconomics', covers the incompatibility of neoclassical theory and macroeconomic theory.

Sources include: Rizvi (1994), Nordhaus and Tobin (1973), Stiglitz et al. (2009), Backhouse (1993, 2002), and Nelson and Winter (1982). The section 'Money-Bargaining and macroeconomics' describes the budgetary and other aspects of the depiction in money-bargaining of macroeconomic processes. The opening section of Chapter 3 (pp. 35–7) is concerned with the history and character of national income accounts, drawing on Backhouse (2002).

The sub-sections 'Home-buyers time shift' and 'Confidence and over-confidence' in Chapter 7 of TEOE, are concerned with the origins of the global financial crisis of 2008. The account derives from Morgenson and Rosner (2012).

The section on 'Neoclassical economic theory and information' in Chapter 4 of EIA covers William Beveridge's (1937) comments on Keynes's *General Theory*. The section on 'Intellectual support-bargaining' in Chapter 2 and the subsection 'Microeconomics and macroeconomics' in Chapter 4 of EIA cover equilibrium research in macroeconomics. Sources include Romer (2016) and Mankiw (2006). This section also includes comment on the wartime development of national income accounts.

Bite 22: Linkages of Support-Bargaining and Money-Bargaining
Chapter 6 of GIR, 'Links Between Money-Bargaining and Support-Bargaining', considers the nature of the bargaining counters and linkages between the two systems. The section 'The subversion of support-bargaining structures' in Chapter 5 also covers interlinks.

The section 'Finance of support-bargaining' in Chapter 2 of SBMDR deals with budgetary interlinks. Part 5 of Chapter 13, 'Financial requirements for a bargaining society', deals with the role of money in the historical emergence of support-bargaining societies. Sources include: Black (1996), Morgan (2001), Pepys (1997), and Pelling (1960).

References

Akerlof, George A., and Shiller, Robert, 2015, *Phishing for Phools*, Princeton University Press.

Akerlof, George A., 1970. 'The Market for "Lemons": Quality Uncertainty and the Market Mechanism', *Quarterly Journal of Economics*, Vol. 84, No. 3, pp. 488–500.

Arrow, Kenneth J., 1950, 'A Difficulty in the Concept of Social Welfare', *Journal of Political Economy*, Vol. 58, No. 4.

Arrow, Kenneth J., 1963, *Social Choice and Individual Values*, Wiley. First published 1951.
Ashton, T. S., 1968/1948, *The Industrial Revolution 1760–1830*, Oxford: Oxford University Press.
Backhouse, Roger E., 1993, *Economists and the Economy: The Evolution of Economic Ideas*, Transaction.
Backhouse, Roger E., 2002, *The Penguin History of Economics*, Penguin.
Bain, J. A., 1954, 'Economies of Scale, Concentration, and the Condition of Entry in Twenty Manufacturing Industries', *American Economic Review*, Vol. 44.
Baumol, William J., 1999, 'Utility and Value' in 'Economic Theory', *Britannica CD*.
Beveridge, William, 1937, 'The Place of the Social Sciences in Human Knowledge', *Politica*, Vol. 2, No. 9, September, pp. 459–79; Farewell Address as Director of the London School of Economics and Political Science, 24 June 1937.
Black, Jeremy, 1996, *A History of the British Isles*, Macmillan.
Blau, Peter, 1964, *Exchange and Power in Social Life*, Wiley, 1964.
Böhm-Bawerk, Eugen von, 1959/1884–1912, *Capital and Interest*, Libertarian Press. First published 1884–1912.
Bruni, Luigino, and Sugden, Robert, 2007, 'The Road Not Taken: How Psychology Was Removed from Economics, and How It Might Be Brought Back', *The Economic Journal*, Vol. 117, No. 516, pp. 146–73.
Buchanan, James, and Tullock, Gordon, 1965, *The Calculus of Consent*, Michigan.
Chamberlin, E. H., 1962/1933, *Theory of Monopolistic Competition*, Oxford University Press, 1962. First published 1933.
Chandler, Alfred, 1977, *The Visible Hand: The Managerial Revolution in American Business*, Belknap Press.
Chandler, Alfred, 1990, *Scale and Scope: The Dynamics of Industrial Capitalism*, Belknap Press.
Chandler, Alfred, 2005, *Inventing the Electronic Century: The Epic Story of the Consumer Electronics and Computer Science Industries*, Harvard University Press.
Clark, John Bates, 1925/1899, *Distribution of Wealth: A Theory of Wages, Interest and Profit*, Macmillan. First published 1899.
Coase, R. H., 1937, 'The Nature of the Firm', *Economica*, New Series, Vol. 4, pp. 386–405.
Coase, R. H., 1960, 'The Problem of Social Cost', *Journal of Law and Economics*, Vol. 3, pp. 1–44.
Coleman, D. C., 1977, *The Economy of England 1450–1750*, Oxford University Press.

Coser, Lewis, 1956, *The Functions of Social Conflict*, Routledge and Kegan Paul.
Crafts, N. F. R., 1986, *British Economic Growth During the Industrial Revolution*, Oxford University Press.
Cyert, R. M., and March, J. G., 1963, *A Behavioural Theory of the Firm*, Prentice-Hall.
Dahrendorf, Ralf, 1959, *Class and Class Conflict in Industrial Society*, Routledge and Kegan Paul.
Davies, Glyn, 1994, *A History of Money from Ancient Times to the Present Day*, University of Wales.
Deane, Phyllis, and Cole, W. A., 1962, *British Economic Growth, 1688–1959*, Cambridge University Press.
Downs, Anthony, 1957, *An Economic Theory of Democracy*, Harper & Row.
Earl, Peter, 1986, *Lifestyle Economics*, St. Martin's Press.
Earl, Peter, 1995, *Microeconomics for Business and Marketing*, Edward Elgar.
Earl, Peter, 2004, 'How Mainstream Economists Model Choice, Versus How We Behave, and Why It Matters', in Fullbrook, 2004.
Friedman, Milton, 1953, 'The Methodology of Positive Economics', in Friedman, Milton, *Essays in Positive Economics*, Chicago: University of Chicago Press.
Fullbrook, Edward (Ed.), 2004, *A Guide to What's Wrong with Economics*, Anthem Press.
Geanakoplos, John, 2004, 'The Arrow-Debreu Model of General Equilibrium', *Cowles Foundation Paper No. 1090*, Cowles Foundation for Research in Economics at Yale University.
Hands, D. W., 2010. 'Economics, Psychology and the History of Consumer Choice Theory', *Cambridge Journal of Economics*, Vol. 34, No. 4.
Heilbroner, Robert L., 1999, 'Adam Smith', *Britannica CD*.
Heilbroner, Robert L., 2017, 'Adam Smith', *Encyclopedia Britannica*, Online, https://www.britannica.com/biography/Adam-Smith. Accessed 18 May 2017.
Hennings, Klaus H., 1986, 'The Exchange Paradigm and the Theory of Production and Distribution', in Baranzini and Scazzieri, 1986.
Hicks, John, 1967, *Critical Essays in Monetary Theory*, Oxford University Press.
Hodgson, Geoffrey, 1988, *Economics and Institutions*, Polity Press.
Hodgson, Geoffrey, 1997, 'The Ubiquity of Habits and Rules', *Cambridge Journal of Economics*, Vol. 21, No. 6, pp. 663–84.
Hodgson, Geoffrey, 2000, *Evolution and Institutions*, Edward Elgar.
Hodgson, Geoffrey, 2006, 'What are Institutions?', *Journal of Economic Issues*, Vol. 40, No. 1, pp. 1–25.
Hotelling, Harold, 1929, 'Stability in Competition', *Economic Journal*, Vol. 39.
Jenner, R. A., 1966, 'An Information Version of Pure Competition', *Economic Journal*, Vol. 76, pp. 786–805; Reprinted in Lamberton, 1971.

Jevons, Stanley, 2013/1871, *The Theory of Political Economy*, Palgrave Macmillan.

Keynes, John Maynard, 1961/1936, *The General Theory of Employment, Interest and Money*, Macmillan. First published 1936.

Kropotkin, Peter, 2003/1902, *Mutual Aid: A Factor of Evolution*, Project Gutenberg Etext, Adobe Digital Editions. First published 1902.

Kuhn, Thomas S., 1970/1962, *The Structure of Scientific Revolutions*, Chicago. First published 1962.

Lamberton, D. M. (Ed.), 1971, *Economics of Information and Knowledge*, Penguin.

Lancaster, Kelvin J., 1966, 'A New Approach to Consumer Theory', *Journal of Political Economy*, Vol. 72, No. 4, pp. 132–57.

Latsis, Spiros J., 1976, 'A research programme in economics', in Latsis, Spiros. J. (Ed.), 1976, *Method and Appraisal in Economics*, Cambridge University Press.

Lindblom, Charles E., 1959, 'The Science of Muddling Through', *Public Administration Review*, Vol 19.

Mankiw, Greg, 2006, 'The Macroeconomist as Scientist and Engineer', *Journal of Economic Perspectives*, Vol. 20, pp. 42–3.

March, James, and Simon, Herbert, 1993/1958, *Organisations*, Blackwell Business. First published 1958.

Marshall, Alfred, 1920/1890, *Principles of Economics*, Eighth Edition, Macmillan. First published 1890.

Martin, John, 1991/1817, *Tonga Islands: William Mariner's Account*, Vava'u Press, Tonga. First published 1817.

Maslow, A. H., 1970/1954, *Motivation and Personality*, Third Edition, Harper & Row. First published 1954.

Mathias, Peter, 2001, *The First Industrial Nation: The Economic History of Britain 1700–1914*, Routledge.

McCloskey, Deirdre N., 2014, 'Measured, Unmeasured, Mismeasured, and Unjustified Pessimism: A Review Essay of Thomas Piketty's Capitalism in the Twenty-First Century', *Erasmus Journal for Philosophy and Economics*, Vol. 7, No. 2, pp. 73–115.

McLeay, Michael, Radia, Amar, and Thomas, Ryland, 2014a, 'Money in the Modern Economy: An Introduction', *Bank of England Quarterly Review*, March 2014, pp. 4–13.

McLeay, Michael, Radia, Amar, and Thomas, Ryland, 2014b, 'Money Creation in the Modern Economy', *Bank of England Quarterly Review*, March 2014, pp. 14–27.

Menger, Karl, 1892, 'On the Origin of Money', *The Economic Journal*, Vol. 2, No. 6.

Menger, Karl, 1950/1871, *Principles of Economics*, Free Press. First published 1871.

Micklethwait, John, and Wooldridge, Adrian, 2005, *The Company: A Short History of a Revolutionary Idea*, Phoenix.

Mill, John Stuart, 1884/1848, *Principles of Political Economy*, Appleton. First published 1848.

Mokyr, Joel, 2011, *The Enlightened Economy: Britain and the Industrial Revolution 1700–1850*, Penguin.

Morgan, Kenneth O. (Ed.), 2001, *The Oxford History of Britain*, Oxford University Press.

Morgenson, Gretchen, and Rosner, Joshua, 2012, *Reckless Endangerment*, St. Martin's Griffin.

Mueller, Dennis C., 1976, 'Public Choice: A Survey', *Journal of Economic Literature*, Vol. 14.

Nelson, Richard R., and Winter, Stanley G., 1982, *An Evolutionary Theory of Economic Change*, Belknap Press.

Nordhaus, William D., and Tobin, James, 1973, 'Is Growth Obsolete?' in *The Measurement of Economic and Social Performance*, National Bureau of Economic Research. http://www.nber.org/chapters/c7620.pdf. Accessed 3 February 2014.

North, Douglass C., 1981, *Structure and Change in Economic History*, Norton.

North, Douglass C., 1990, *Institutions, Institutional Change and Economic Performance*, Cambridge University Press.

Pelling, Henry, 1960, *Modern Britain, 1885–1955*, Nelson.

Pepys, Samuel, 1997, *The Concise Pepys*, Wordsworth.

Pigou, Arthur C., 1932, *The Economics of Welfare*, Macmillan.

Pigou, Arthur C., 1933, *The Theory of Unemployment*, Macmillan.

Piketty, Thomas, 2014, *Capital in the 21st Century*, tr. Arthur Goldhammer, Belknap Press.

Ricardo, David, 2010/1817, *On the Principles of Political Economy and Taxation*, Project Gutenberg EBook (Murray, 1817). First published 1817.

Richardson, George B., 1990/1960, *Information and Investment: A Study in the Working of the Competitive Economy*, Second Edition, Oxford University Press. First published 1960.

Rizvi, S. Abu Turab, 1994, 'The Microfoundations Project in General Equilibrium Theory', *Cambridge Journal of Economics*, Vol. 18, No. 4, pp. 357–77.

Robbins, Lionel, 1932, *An Essay on the Nature and Significance of Economic Science*, Macmillan.

Robinson, Joan, 1979/1933, *The Economics of Imperfect Competition*, Macmillan. First published 1933.

Romer, Paul, 2016, 'The Trouble with Macroeconomics', Lecture, delivered January 5, 2016 as the Commons Memorial Lecture of the Omicron Delta

Epsilon Society. https://paulromer.net/wp-content/uploads/2016/09/WP-Trouble.pdf. Accessed 27 April 2017.

Rose, Jonathan, 2002, *The Intellectual Life of the British Working Classes*, Yale Nota Bene.

Schumpeter, Joseph A. 1954/1942, *Capitalism, Socialism and Democracy*, Unwin. First published 1942.

Searle, John, 1996, *The Construction of Social Reality*, Penguin.

Sen, A, 1984, *Resources, Value and Development*, Blackwell.

Simon, Herbert A., 1997/1947, *Administrative Behaviour: A Study of Decision-Making Processes in Administrative Organizations*, Free Press. First published 1947.

Smith, Adam, 1976/1759, *The Theory of Moral Sentiments*, Clarendon Press. First published 1759.

Smith, Adam, 2009/1776, *An Enquiry into the Nature and Causes of the Wealth of Nations*, Adobe Digital Editions. First published 1776.

Spread, Patrick, 1984, *A Theory of Support and Money Bargaining* (TSMB), Macmillan.

Spread, Patrick, 2004, *Getting It Right: Economics and the Security of Support* (GIR), Book Guild.

Spread, Patrick, 2008, *Support-Bargaining: The Mechanics of Democracy Revealed* (SBMDR), Book Guild.

Spread, Patrick, 2011, 'Situation as Determinant of Selection and Valuation', *Cambridge Journal of Economics*, Vol. 35, No. 2. Reprinted in Spread, 2015b.

Spread, Patrick, 2013, *Support-Bargaining, Economics and Society: A Social Species* (SBES), Routledge.

Spread, Patrick, 2015a, 'Asymmetric Information, Critical Information and the Information Interface', *Real-World Economics Review*, Issue 70, pp. 121–40. Reprinted in Spread, 2015b.

Spread, Patrick, 2016a, *The Evolution of Economies: Money-Bargaining, Economic Change and Industrial Revolution (TEOE)*, Routledge.

Spread, Patrick, 2016b, 'Companies and Markets: Economic Theories of the Firm and a Concept of Companies as Bargaining Agencies', *Cambridge Journal of Economics*, Vol. 40, No. 3, pp. 727–53. Reprinted in Spread, 2015b.

Spread, Patrick, 2019, *Economics for an Information Age: Money-Bargaining, Support-Bargaining and the Information Interface (EIA)*, Routledge.

Stigler, G. J., 1961, 'The Economics of Information', *Journal of Political Economy*, Vol. 69, pp. 213–25. Reprinted in Lamberton, 1971.

Stiglitz, Joseph E., Sen, Amartya and Fitoussi, Jean-Paul, 2009, Report by the Commission on the Measurement of Economic Performance and Social Progress. http://www.stiglitz-sen-fitoussi.fr/documents/rapport_anglais.pdf. Accessed 3 February 2014.

Thibaut, John and Kelly, Harold, 1959, *The Social Psychology of Groups*, Wiley.
Thompson, E. P., 1991/1963, *The Making of the English Working Class*, Penguin. First published 1963.
Thornton, Henry, 1802, *An Enquiry into the Nature and Effects of the Paper Credit of Great Britain*, J. Hatchard.
Veblen, T., 1994/1899, *Theory of the Leisure Class*, Penguin. First published 1899.
Walras, Leon, 2003/1874, *Elements of Pure Economics: Or, The Theory of Social Wealth*, Routledge. First published 1874.
Weber, Max, 1949, *The Methodology of the Social Sciences*, Free Press. Essays written 1903–17.
Wildavsky, Aaron, 1964, *The Politics of the Budgetary Process*, Little, Brown.
Williamson, O. E., 1975. *Markets and Hierarchies: Analysis and Antitrust Implications: A Study in the Economics of Internal Organization*, Free Press.
Wrigley, E. A. and Schofield, R. S., 1981, *The Population History of England, 1541–1871: A Reconstruction*, Cambridge University Press.
Wrigley, E. A., 2010, *Energy and the English Industrial Revolution*, Cambridge University Press.

CHAPTER 6

Information

Abstract The recognition of support-bargaining and money-bargaining as basic to the functioning of societies involves recognition also of the role of information. Transactions are evaluated on the basis of information, but beyond that, our whole experience is based on information. Our minds only deal with information. Information is used not so much in pursuit of truth as for the advance of interests in transactions of support-bargaining and money-bargaining. Information is codified for transmission. Neoclassical economic theory has subordinated its concepts to the requirements of mathematical codification. Media organisations disseminate information that affects the distribution of support, giving them an active and essential role in the process of government. The impossibility of identifying truth has meant that people develop localised understanding in their different spheres of what will constitute truth adequate to their purpose.

Keywords Information · Pursuit of truth · Codification · Media organisations · External world · Scientific method

Bite 23: Information and the Information Interface

In support-bargaining and money-bargaining, social and political relationships are conceived as networks of bargaining transactions. Something is provided for something received. What is provided depends

P. Spread, *A Starter on Support-Bargaining and Money-Bargaining in Twenty-Eight Digestible Bites*,
https://doi.org/10.1007/978-3-030-05231-7_6

on the capacity of the provider. The relevance, usefulness and valuation of whatever is received depend on an assessment of its fit to situation. Information defines what is received and the situation to which it fits. The terms of transactions depend on bargaining position, as described in Bite 17. To fully establish bargaining position, agents need information not only about their own situation and requirements, but about the situations and interests of their counterpart agents, including the alternatives open to each.

But the role of information goes deeper. Transactions are conceived and realised in the form of information. It is not a question of dealing in something, whether ideas or potatoes, and having information about its value, availability and the terms of exchange; information constitutes the whole matter. The 'something' is itself a matter of information. Our minds deal only with information, so anything we deal with has to come in the form of information. This includes the transactions of support-bargaining and money-bargaining, which constitute the essential part of human social interaction. It is therefore necessary to take account of the way human minds seek, select, interpret, organise, codify and transmit information.

This information centred understanding of the process of support-bargaining and money-bargaining gives rise to the concept of an information interface in which the process is conducted. Rather than dealing with an 'external world', we deal with information assembled in an information interface. Crucially, the information interface is easily manipulated. The interface is created as part of the social bargaining process, involving manipulation of information for bargaining advantage. Most prominently, agents endeavour to establish in the information interface the frames of reference, situation concepts and 'stories' that will dispose others to perceive and interpret in ways conducive to the interests of the creating agents. What is beyond the information interface is only a matter of conjecture, and conjecture which is necessarily itself only a part of the information interface. We live in an information interface. We contribute to the information interface for the advance of our interests and conduct our business by reference to the information it contains.

The information interface will evolve over time in reaction to the emergence of new information. Part of this new information will be related to changing situations and interests arising from outcomes of transactions just concluded. We learn by experience. The outcomes of transactions, what we experience as a result of buying a house or a car, will become known to us in the form of information. We compare the information we gain from experiencing the outcome of a transaction with the expectations we had in agreeing the transaction, and conclude that we got a good deal, or were swindled, or could have done better. The new information will form part of the evolving information interface.

While it will be readily accepted that we are confined to what is in our minds, and hence can deal only with information, this understanding of the relationship of humans with the world around them is contrary to the understanding of common theory and the understanding of information in common theory. Information is regarded in common theory as being 'about' something, whether it be the state of the roads, the condition of a refrigerator or some abstract idea. At least in the case of roads and the refrigerator, the 'something' is conceived as existing independently of the conception of it and the information about it. 'Good information' is information that accurately portrays what it is about; 'bad information' is information that is inaccurate or misleading with regard to the 'true' nature of what it is about. 'Bad people' may deceive others for their own ends about the true nature of things; 'good people' acknowledge their obligations to their society and try to be truthful. The formal theoretical extensions of common theory generally have the same understanding of the existence of an external world and the nature of information about it.

The traditional understanding of a world external to our minds includes also an understanding that we can have access to it through information. Compiling accurate information will tell us about the external world. Gaining information and knowledge is gaining information and knowledge about this external world. The 'pursuit of truth' is traditionally the search for understanding of the external world. The most common understanding of access to the external world is that it is a matter of divine revelation. The dominance of deity theory has been an important factor in the understanding of what information and knowledge can be acquired. Latterly, the natural sciences have seemed to provide dependable information about the external world. Methodical elimination of any influence of non-truth interests is taken to leave only truth about the external world (Bite 13). But in terms of the understanding of information in support-bargaining and money-bargaining, such information only adds to an information interface that is the limit of our knowledge. We can never reach beyond the capacities of our minds, though we may recognise the consistencies in an information interface that lend themselves to explanations in terms of the probability of a world independent of our minds. Post-modern philosophers ram home the point that probability is not conclusive proof.

In the idea of support-bargaining and money-bargaining, information is the focus of attention. It creates and shapes the transactions that are undertaken. The support-bargaining and money-bargaining process gains much of its character from the malleability of information. Information is moulded for the advance of interests in social bargaining. Much of the competition in a social bargaining system involves efforts to establish certain information as prominent and essential, and certain other information as erroneous and misleading. 'Follow my frame of reference and you will see things in their true light; follow that other frame of reference and you will be lost'. In money-bargaining: 'The car I am selling will meet all your requirements, being fast, comfortable, reliable, safe, prestigious and a bargain; those of my competitors are overpriced junk'. Whether cultivating support with a view to social ascendancy or accumulating money with a view to wealth, ensuring the prominence and acceptance of supportive information, whilst eliminating or discrediting unhelpful information, are crucial to success. Word selection plays a major role in the manipulation of information. Every frame of reference has its associated vocabulary.

The significance of information only becomes apparent with the recognition of support-bargaining and money-bargaining as the common transactional basis of human society. Support-bargaining and money-bargaining provides a frame of reference in which the role of information comes sharply into focus. As was seen in Bite 8, democracy conceives only of debate generating a vague 'general good'. Bite 9 suggests that one of the primary functions of political parties, themselves inimical to democratic principles, is to disseminate information in a form that will raise support for the party. Economic theory assumes with common theory that we deal directly with 'reality' as external phenomena. Perception is perception of things as they are, not perception of information about them. Experience is experience of actual events, not the receipt of information pertaining to experience. Support-bargaining, more than money-bargaining, deals with abstractions. In support-bargaining, it is plain that we are very often dealing with information relating to concepts and ideas that have no other being than through the information that describes them. Then it becomes apparent also that economic transactions are matters of information. We do not deal with 'things' of an external world, but with information that we suppose is about the things of an external world. The information we receive is selective, being confined to features of supposed things that are relevant to our situation. Through information, we become aware of the potential for transactions. We are bounded by an information interface and do what we can to mould it to our advantage, or evaluate it in such a way as to discern what is to our advantage.

Bite 24: Information in a Bargaining System

The idea of support-bargaining and money-bargaining involves a change in concerns over information from the traditional understanding of gaining information about an external world to an understanding based on the role of information in a bargaining system. Eternal verities cease to be of much account; the concern is with the dissemination of information that is likely to advance interests in a bargaining system, and the acquisition of information that will ensure the maximum advantage from transactions.

As was seen in Bite 12 and in the previous bite, one essential for the advance of interests in a social and political context through the use of information is the creation of 'frames of reference' that cause people to observe selectively and understand what they observe in accordance with the interests it is desired to advance. The frames of reference may be the elaborate theories of society created or developed in universities, such as socialism, liberalism, neoclassical economic theory, communism, institutional economic theory and so on. These are formulated and agreed through the process of intellectual support-bargaining described in Bites 10–13. But references may also be more modest constructions, such as local deficiencies in transport services.

Political support-bargaining involves professional engagement in the assembly of support. It is vitally important to politicians that the information interface has the sort of content that will cause people to give support to their cause. Political factions on the right ensure that the information interface is full of material showing how the freedom of individuals brings benefits to society as a whole. Those campaigning for support in a rural area may disseminate information regarding the value of rural conservation. In money-bargaining also people are professionally involved in ensuring that the information interface is full of information conducive to their interests. A company selling furniture will want to ensure that potential buyers know the particular features of the company's products that make them well-suited to their situations, and preferable to the products of all other companies.

The recipients of such political and commercial information have to evaluate the information to ascertain their own advantage. Where circumstances permit—that is, within the limitations imposed by their situation—they are likely to seek other sources of information, potentially less committed to the advance of a particular cause, or committed to the advance of a different cause. They must then assess what will 'best fit' their situation, either with regard to a transaction of money-bargaining (Bite 15) or with regard to political advantage (Bite 3).

The 'other sources' perform a function analogous to that of replicative testing in the natural sciences (Bite 13). They provide a test of the consistency of different sources of information, and hence a guide to what is most likely to be trustworthy with regard to the outcomes of different transactions. In the political context, people tend to be aware that information provided is likely to be heavily manipulated for the assembly of support. The general and abstract nature of the information provided rules out any rigorous testing, such as can be pursued with the more stable phenomena of natural scientific enquiry. People tend to determine what they will accept by reference to past experience. They tend to trust people whom they regard as being in a similar situation to themselves, and hence sharing their interests. In the context of money-bargaining, the durable nature of products makes possible rigorous testing of products more in accordance with the principles of natural scientific testing. Consumer organisations provide information on the qualities of products based on systematic testing of products and systematic evaluation of the performance of suppliers.

Acceptance of information depends also on the form in which it is received. Much of the information which defines and evaluates transactions in a support-bargaining and money-bargaining system is testimonial information—that is, information derived from other agents of a bargaining system rather than information directly accessed by personal perception. Testimonial information is inevitably shaped by the interests of the testifier. The public information interface is comprised of testimonial information manipulated in accordance with the interests of its contributors. Direct perceptual information is nevertheless common in money-bargaining. People go out and inspect what they are buying. Even transactions made over the internet on the basis of testimonial information can normally be rejected on the basis of direct perceptual information obtained after delivery. In political and social support-bargaining, direct perception plays a lesser role. People may be familiar with the state of the roads in their immediate neighbourhood, but any broader comprehension, relating to a national network, depends on testimonial information. Information on policies is largely abstract and so necessarily testimonial.

Perceptual information is generally more convincing than testimonial information. Perceptual information belongs to the perceiver alone, without contamination from the interests of others. The sense of conviction associated with perception may be related to the necessity of dependable perceptual information to the survival of the species. In violent times, survival may depend on instantaneous reaction to certain sights and sounds. The perceptual information received must be received with the instantaneous conviction necessary to action. Only those that have dependable perceptions and depend on their perceptions will survive. There is a long-standing tradition in philosophy that perception gives undeniably true knowledge.

The conviction arising from perception may be attributed also to the ease with which we exercise perceptual faculties. Psychological tests reveal that 'cognitive ease' is an important determinant of the conviction we attach to information. For example, we assimilate rhyming information with greater conviction than we assimilate similar information without the rhyme. Perceptual information is in general more easily assimilated than testimonial information. Testimonial information demands cognitive effort.

While 'cognitive ease' helps to explain the conviction attaching to perceptual information, it also suggests that some testimonial information will be accepted with similar conviction. People raised in a certain faith receive with cognitive ease and corresponding conviction information provided in the context of that faith. Such people learning that a child has been saved from a house brought down in an earthquake will be convinced that such salvation is attributable to the mercy of god, without regard for the origins of the earthquake. Testimonial information that has reference to frames of reference in which people have been raised is likely to be accepted with conviction of comparable strength to that experienced through direct perceptual information. The conviction attaching to interpretations of faith may have conditioned people to acceptance or tolerance of interpretations related to particular frames of reference that are wildly inconsistent with interpretations of common theory.

The conviction attaching to perceptual information is not always justified. Information obtained by systematic measurement sometimes shows that the convictions of perception are inconsistent with the information derived from measurement. 'Illusion' is most commonly demonstrated in books on perception by pictures involving deceptive contrasts of scale or distorted perspective. The perplexity experienced over revealed illusion is a measure of the strength of initial conviction. Such 'illusions' provide information about the nature of perception and the working of human minds. They demonstrate that perception is not wholly reliable, but they scarcely discourage people from trusting their perceptions in the normal run of their affairs.

Perceptual and testimonial information seem easily distinguished. But the advance of technology for the transmission of information means that the distinction is no longer as plain as it was. Perception implied that the perceivers were seeing or hearing phenomena that directly confronted them. It meant that they were in close contact with whatever was perceived. Testimonial information implied that the information referred to phenomena that were distant from the recipient. That has changed with advances in the technology for the codification and transmission of information. Modern technology permits transmission of testimonial information in a perceptual form that may stimulate conviction comparable to that of direct perception. People watch and hear films using their senses of perception, though what they receive is testimonial information. They cry, wince and become fearful as if they had direct perception of the phenomena represented. There is such 'cognitive ease' that representations on film can be assimilated with a conviction that is unwarranted. It requires cognitive effort, conscious analysis, and a positive inclination, to distinguish the testimonial status of film from the perceptual status of the information actually received, and hence to withhold the conviction that is instinctively attached to perceptual information. Advances in 'virtual reality' are likely to confuse even further the difference in character between perceptual and testimonial information and hence make it more difficult to distinguish what is invented from what is 'real'. Such opportunities for manipulation suggest that the information interface is likely to become yet more infused with misleading and false information.

Bite 25: Codification and Transmission of Information

Our minds deal only with information. But communication between people requires that information is put into a form in which it can be transmitted and received. Information is codified for transmission. The relationship between 'raw' information and codified information is not simple. Communication is so fundamental to humans that information itself seems closely bound up with its codified forms. It is nevertheless possible to conceive 'raw' information as the perceptual impressions of what we encounter, and sensations that we derive from contemplating such impressions in our minds. We assimilate large amounts of information every day, only a small part of which is codified for communication. We experience sensations of fear, attraction and pleasure from our perceptions which are recognised without codification. Ideas, if only vague ideas, may also be present in the mind in uncodified form. People have ideas and concepts in their minds that they do not express in language.

Codification takes various forms. 'Body language' and touching are highly instinctive communications, often conveying the highly instinctive sensations of aversion, threat, antagonism, protection, sympathy and attraction. These instinctive expressions have less of the element of artificiality, of one thing standing for another, than is implicit in the notion of codification. Nevertheless, certain body movements are instinctively understood as conveying certain sentiments, and the same body movements may be used consciously to impress sentiments on others. Body language is expressive but limited in the range of information it can convey.

Language is the most common form of codification in the information interface. Specialists in linguistics suggest that capacity for language is an integral part of human biological evolution and hence closely integrated with the 'raw' information that we have in our minds. Language makes possible the communication of complex ideas and instructions between humans. Given the prominence of support-bargaining in human relations, it would be surprising if language were not well-adapted for social bargaining. The variety of words and grammatical constructions in languages that can be associated with the assembly of support suggests that language has evolved for support-bargaining. It might almost be said that using language is taking sides. Every frame of reference has its vocabulary (Bites 1 and 23). Using words is then adopting a frame of reference.

Since linguistic communication requires that both the initiator and receiver share the same code, language also facilitates and impedes the formation of groups. Nation states derive much of their rigidity from the use of a common language amongst their people, largely excluding those who do not share the language from the internal national support-bargaining. The difficulties of integrating European nation states into a single union have been compounded by the linguistic divisions that are largely coterminous with the states.

The potency of language as a means of communication was enhanced by the invention of written language, apparently introduced to the world by Sumerians around 3200 BC. The earliest example of writing in Europe was found in Greece on a tablet dated to about 1500 BC. In Britain, the earliest writing was found in 2016 near the Bank tube station in London. An inscribed tablet, fittingly about finance, has been dated to 43 AD, the start of the Roman occupation. The Romans were able to communicate with each other in writing, while there is no evidence that the Celts could do so. Communication in writing is more copious and effective across space and time than oral transmission. The information interface in which intellectual support-bargaining is conducted is heavily dependent on written communications. A textual information interface forms the basis of legal systems established through political support-bargaining.

Writing was hand-writing in Europe up to the introduction of the Gutenberg printing press in the fifteenth century. The press made feasible the format of companies to print and publish written material. Low unit costs made possible low prices and high levels of sales. The technology was of central importance to the mobilisation of support for the religious disputes and the violence of the Reformation. Steam-driven presses later made possible longer print runs and yet lower unit costs, which, with the railways offering means of bulk transportation of printed material, made possible the dissemination of the copious information necessary to an industrial revolution. The codification of information in language has moved in the past few decades to digital codification, setting in train transformations in society comparable to those of the earlier technical innovations.

For many centuries, the skills of reading and writing were confined to very few. Those who had such skills formed a distinct 'learned' social group engaged in the intellectual support-bargaining that assembled support for certain ways of thinking and courses of action. They had extensive influence on the evolution of their societies. Illiterate people were and are substantially dependent on the literate.

Different modes of codification affect the information that is communicated. Linguistic codification provides the most varied and extensive opportunities for influencing what is communicated. Languages have developed to convey a wide range of activity and thought in very subtle ways. Words acquire through usage certain sympathies that influence the assembly of support. Understanding language is not just a matter of meaning in any neutral sense, but of interpreting also the sympathies of words. Grammatical forms also influence the sort of information that is conveyed. There is 'cognitive ease' in the use of familiar grammatical forms, such as the 'subject-noun...active-verb' construction. The ease of use of this grammatical form has led to the potentially misleading personification of inanimate phenomena. 'Nature selects her survivors' is easily said and easily assimilated, but it does not provide accurate information about the process of natural selection.

Language depends on memory and analytical capacities, rather than perceptual capacities. Other forms of codification are matters of perceptual representation and reception. Pictures, sculpture, music, photography and film all depend on perceptual faculties. Besides their straightforward representational content, these perceptual forms of communication involve an important element of symmetry. The symmetry of rhyme facilitates the assimilation of written information, and the spatial symmetries of images facilitate the assimilation of the information conveyed by pictures. Music plays with aural symmetries, conveying to the receptive various emotional experiences, often echoed in words accompanying music, or in the symmetries of dance.

Information is also coded mathematically. This is the most precise form of codification, though amongst the most limited. Its use is confined to certain concepts that have the requisite characteristics. Some people have particular facility and fascination with mathematics itself, independently of its function in the communication of information. In the natural sciences, the use of mathematics has been extraordinarily fruitful. In the social sciences, its use has also been highly advantageous. With regard to microeconomic transactions, however, it has been applied with such little concern for its limitations that it has proved highly misleading.

As reviewed in Bite 18, mathematical economists have established an 'economic model', a mathematical account of microeconomic transactions, which forms the 'mainstream' of economic understanding and instruction. The dominance of the model and its theory group in universities ensures its transmission from generation to generation. Those within the theory group have the advantages of institutionalised ascendancy. Their mathematical prowess is comparatively rare. Their bargaining position is analogous to that established through institutionalisation of those skilled in reading and writing at a time when such accomplishments were rare. Mathematical skills have not been uniformly accompanied by understanding of information derived from observation and experience of the conduct of economic exchange.

While all modes of codification influence the information that is communicated, the influence of mathematical codification goes deeper. The concepts of 'mainstream' economic theory are subordinated to the requirements of mathematical codification. Instead of the codes being used to communicate information developed independently, the requirements for mathematical codification are allowed to dictate the concepts adopted. The model is conceived in a 'mathematical dimension', outside the time and space of common encounter. Mathematical codification requires that the phenomena of interest should have features that are amenable to quantification and potentially related in ways that can be modelled mathematically. Economic activity seems at first sight admirably suited to mathematical codification, since it apparently deals largely with 'products' that are distinct and countable. But the products are in reality highly varied, and there are people involved. The practice has been for economists, finding that phenomena do not demonstrate the required characteristics, redefine the phenomena so that they do.

This redefining for mathematical convenience is apparent in the neoclassical concept of 'products' as uniform, not differentiated by features that fit them to different consumer situations. A shirt has to be a shirt, and not a shirt with long sleeves or short sleeves, in different colours and sizes, sold in different locations. Only with this understanding is it possible to conceive the 'supply' and 'demand' schedules that determine a 'market price'.

Similar redefining is apparent in the treatment by George Akerlof of one of the factors, quality, that distinguishes products of the same type. George Stigler draws attention to the difficulties of specifying 'quality', but Akerlof reduces average 'quality' to μ (mu), with the 'quality' of the *i*'th car as x_i, and provides a mathematical analysis of the significance of 'quality' in terms of these two variables. He acknowledges that his treatment of 'quality' is entirely unrealistic, but gives no reason why he thinks it useful to provide an unrealistic account of quality. The usefulness of such analysis to himself is nevertheless apparent in the acclaim of the theory group. They take it that he has resolved a difficulty of the neoclassical model concerning 'quality', and such service to the theory group merits reward. It is a matter of intellectual support-bargaining within a theory group.

The same propensity to redefine phenomena in accordance with mathematical requirements is apparent in the neoclassical understanding of 'people'. 'People' are to a degree unpredictable in their behaviour. 'Human volition' makes social science difficult to pursue with the same methods as are used in the natural sciences. To accommodate humanity in the mathematical model, economists opt to incorporate in their model the one particular feature of human behaviour, the rational element, directed towards material ends, that is convenient to mathematical analysis (Bite 13). Humans become more predictable, more uniform, in a way that lends itself to mathematical modelling. People in the round are effectively excluded from the codified understanding of economic exchange. The demands of mathematical codification impose a particular view of economic transactions which is seriously misleading (Bites 13 and 18).

Pictures, including paintings, drawings and photographs, are influential through the selections they impose on transmission and the sympathies they can evoke through their portrayals of human and other circumstances. If words are persuasive, so too, and more, are pictures. Television news and documentary films provide perceptual experiences that are remarkably 'true to life' and hence arouse strong convictions, but nevertheless involve selection and presentation of phenomena according to the interests of their makers. Makers of film dramas add to this verisimilitude the narrative forms that make oral and textual stories so compelling (Bite 10). The internet has opened new opportunities for the dissemination of information in film. 'The medium' is not 'the message', as Marshall McLuhan argued. The technology of film making does not make the medium important regardless of the information it conveys. The medium is important because, as was seen in the previous bite, it makes it possible to convey testimonial information in the form of perceptual information. Codification in film provides information that is received with the special conviction of perceptual information. While film is well-suited to the conveyance of perceptual information, it has limited capacity to convey information of a more analytical kind.

Film is also highly accessible. Both linguistic and mathematical codifications involve restricted reception of the information they convey. People have to be able to read, or understand mathematics. Those lacking the relevant skills are cut off from information codified in these forms. With film, however, the information can be received by almost everyone, so that almost everyone feels they have the necessary information to engage in support-bargaining. People form opinions on any subject, often with great conviction, on the basis of what they encounter in films, on television and on the internet.

Transmission of information is for the most part a separate operation from that of codification. With the spoken word, codification is mostly concurrent with transmission, but written language, whether hand-written, printed or digitally encoded, has to be transmitted separately. Television, though it may be 'live', involves discernibly distinct processes of filming and transmitting. The generally distinct requirement for transmission of print, digitally encoded material, film, internet communications and other codified information has given rise to establishment of a network of transmission comparable in function and social importance to physical transport infrastructures. In some cases, the information infrastructure has ridden on the back of the transport infrastructure. Roads and tracks have always provided means for the transmission of information, as well as goods and people. The construction of railways around Europe from around 1830 provided means for the carriage of newspapers, opening opportunities for the establishment of viable companies disseminating information on a substantial scale. In this way, perhaps as much as their opening of opportunities for companies formatting for the provision of goods, the railways extended money-bargaining. People became better informed about the goods and services available and how to get them. The wider availability of political information played an essential part in the transformation of societies in the nineteenth century.

While in the early stages the information infrastructure depended on the transport infrastructure, technological innovations gave it its own distinct forms. Companies formatted for the provision of telegraphic and wireless transmission of information. The present information infrastructure involves a wide range of cable, terrestrial wireless and satellite communications systems. Unprecedented volumes of information can be transmitted around the world at very low cost.

The importance of the information infrastructure, including in particular the impact of the Gutenberg press and the introduction of digital communications, is generally well recognised in accounts of social change. The accounts are, however, notably lacking in any theoretical framework by which to understand the significance of information. Neither democratic theory (Bite 8) nor economic theory (Bites 18 and 26) offers any reference by which the role of information can be understood. It is only with the theory of support-bargaining and money-bargaining, and the identification of an essential role for information (Bite 23), that the significance of an information infrastructure and its usage can be given a satisfactory theoretical context.

Bite 26: Information in Money-Bargaining

Money-bargaining transactions are conceived, negotiated and their outcomes experienced as information. Hence an understanding of the function of information is important to the understanding of money-bargaining. While participants may generally be said to recognise the importance of information, the basic formulation of the neoclassical economic model avoids the issue with an assumption that all necessary information is available. Good and free information, as much as is required, which is very little in the mainstream model, is available. Mathematical codification cannot accommodate the confusion implicit in an uneven distribution and wholesale manipulation of information.

Information issues are nevertheless so prominent that even neoclassical economists have not been able to ignore them entirely. Since the 1960s, an 'economics of information' has attempted to reconcile observed functions of information with the neoclassical model. Some writers recognise explicitly that information issues cannot be satisfactorily reconciled with the model. As with other extensions aimed at reconciling information derived from observation and experience with the model, information issues make plain the dysfunction of the basic model. But for the most part, it is concluded within the theory group that information issues require no more than modifications to the basic concepts of the model.

The main modification is that of 'asymmetric information'. Akerlof's account of 'quality', referred to in the previous bite, is presented as a matter of 'asymmetric information'—the sellers of motor vehicles know the qualities of their vehicles while potential buyers do not. More generally, the incidence of 'asymmetric information'—some people in a money-bargaining system know more than others—has been accepted as a satisfactory accommodation of information issues. 'Markets' deal with asymmetric information through guarantees, cultivation of reputation and the use of brand names. Few people will be surprised to learn that some people are better informed than others, but to neoclassical economists, who start from the assumption that all necessary information is available, it is a revelation.

Following Akerlof, the idea of 'asymmetric information' has been developed most prominently by Joseph Stiglitz. He does not, however, accept that information issues can be reconciled with the neoclassical model through the idea of 'asymmetric information'. Rather, he recognises the incompatibility. He advocates a 'paradigm change'—the replacement of the neoclassical model by a theory that can satisfactorily accommodate the idea that some people are better informed than others. He nevertheless chooses to continue working within the paradigm of the neoclassical model, treating 'asymmetric information' as mere modification. He argues that those who dominate the mainstream theory group are so resistant to change that is it not worth bothering with change. It is more comfortable to cultivate support within the dominant theory group.

George Akerlof and Robert Shiller have recently made a further attempt to reconcile information issues with the neoclassical model. In *Phishing for Phools*, they provide an extensive and detailed account of the manipulation of information in economic transactions in pursuit of economic interests. Yet, they conclude that it is all perfectly compatible with the basic neoclassical model. All that is required is a minor modification: the 'optimal allocation of resources' that is the most fundamentally attractive quality of the model has to be understood as optimal allocation on the basis of the information made available to buyers. That it is an optimal allocation of fools is of no account. It is an example of the dogmatic, quasi-religious, attachment to the model characteristic of neoclassical economists. The model is sacrosanct within the theory group. It is also a matter of 'politics', in that the ascendancy of the theory group depends in large part on the cohesion of the group. Those involved in intellectual support-bargaining manoeuvre for cohesive support in the same way as politicians. Like Stiglitz, Akerlof and Shiller see no advantage in displacing the dominant theory group. The theory group sets loyalty above sound theory.

The manipulation of information on which decisions to buy are made, as described by Akerlof and Shiller, means that 'products' no longer have the uniformity that is necessary to mathematical codification. Every buyer receives extensive manipulated information and selects some part of it, interpreting it as well as can be done, as the basis of a decision. Every buyer recognises something different in what he or she buys. Rational humans, as conceived in the neoclassical model, have the same accurate information about their purchases and make their decisions on the basis of that information. But fools all assimilate different information and make their decisions on that different information. All buy on the basis of a different understanding of what they are buying, so that every transaction is unique. There is no compatibility with the basic model. *Phishing for Phools* overlays the neoclassical model with manipulated information without regard for the incongruity.

Akerlof and Shiller at least recognise that there is more to the problem of information than just some people being better informed than others. It was seen in Bite 15 that consumers buy by reference to their situations. They assemble information to form a 'bargaining set' comprising those products or services, or their suppliers, that meet the constraints imposed by situation. Since each consumer creates an individual understanding of situation, each decision is unique. An acquisition has to fit a situation, physically, aesthetically and in terms of a budget. Consumers may be fools and they may be fooled, but they try to achieve a 'best fit' with their situation as they define it.

In Bite 16, it was seen that companies seeking to meet the viability condition develop products with features that they anticipate will fit the situations of a sufficient number of buyers to give them the revenues they need to meet the viability condition. They disseminate copious information designed to convince potential buyers that the features available with their products are just those that will fit their situation. High disparity between the information disseminated to promote sales and information derived from post-purchase experience of a product will, however, erode confidence in a company's products and threaten sales. Ethical and legal considerations further ensure that information is manipulated for the most part within limits of social tolerance.

The dissemination of information is achieved through advertising in newspapers and magazines, on television and on the internet. Decorative window displays, promotional articles, prize draws and many other devices further disseminate information favourable to acceptance of a company's products and services. Outside the consumer context, for example in contemplation of major investments, companies will undertake extensive and expensive research to assemble information relevant to their acquisitions. Money-bargaining transactions take place through an information interface, and much effort is expended in creating the information interface in a form conducive to the interests of its creators.

While the neoclassical economic model is solely concerned with individual interests, actual money-bargaining systems accommodate a wide range of communal interests, mostly through the agency of government (Bite 20). The identification of communal interests is a matter of support-bargaining, involving copious assembly and dispute over information. The major role of political support-bargaining can be seen as the identification of communal interest and the establishment of budgets through which communal interest can be advanced. The importance of information in support-bargaining and money-bargaining societies is recognised in communal provision for education (Bite 19).

'Information' is sometimes treated as a 'commodity' or 'product' subject to a dynamic of supply and demand similar to that of the neoclassical model. 'Information' is, however, the polar opposite of the uniform 'products' of the neoclassical model. Information is almost infinitely malleable. It is, in effect, an extreme type of 'product' as conceived in the idea of money-bargaining. In money-bargaining, companies endow products with features intended to fit them to the situations of potential buyers. When information is to be sold, it is shaped to fit the interests of potential buyers. The media sell information that will appeal to their readers (Bite 27). Conceived as a product, information is like a key that unlocks transactions in other products. Like a key, it is specific to particular circumstances. A key will unlock doors that it is made to unlock. Keys have something of the specificity of information. Information unlocks transactions that it is designed to unlock, or locks up transactions which might otherwise be open. While an agent of a bargaining system will not normally want to disseminate his product freely—a farmer will not bombard his customers with potatoes—an agent will want to provide potential customers with the 'key' that unlocks transactions in his own products.

The scope for dissemination of misinformation or misleading information about products and services by companies competing for sales has resulted in the establishment through support-bargaining of a large body of regulations to which companies must conform in their efforts to gain acceptance of their output. These regulations protect buyers against misleading information, and in some cases protect companies providing services, such as insurance, on the basis of information provided by buyers. They have had the effect of raising confidence in the efficacy of money-bargaining in advancing people's interests, and have consequently facilitated growth of money-bargaining systems.

Bite 27: Role of Media in Governance

The main agencies disseminating information to the information interface for political support-bargaining and money-bargaining are information media—newspapers, magazines, radio, television, internet companies. Very few people have direct access to those who make political decisions and their speeches. No one can check all the outcomes of government programmes. Most people depend on the media for the information on which they base their decisions to support one political faction or another. Even those actively involved in political processes have direct access only to a small part of proceedings. For the rest, they depend largely on media reports. The media consequently have a major role in the governance of a society. Collectively, they determine what information reaches the general public, and in what form, and hence the sort of political transactions that can be concluded. Bite 11 touched on their role in the context of intellectual support-bargaining.

The media in Britain consist mostly of money-bargaining organisations formatted for the dissemination of information. Their first concern is consequently to provide themselves with the revenues necessary to viability (Bite 16). They provide information that people will buy; they disseminate information that other organisations will pay to have disseminated. People buy information that is relevant to their interests. The information has to contribute to the formation of the situation-related bargaining sets through which buyers make decisions on purchases (Bite 15). It is found that the more factual and less partisan type of political information sells in relatively small volume. People concerned with detailed political information and analysis form a relatively small part of populations. Most will pay only for information that is lively to the point of sensational. Relevance is commonly maintained through a focus on the personal and the alarming.

The emergence of the internet as a major means of disseminating information and a major source of information of all kinds is recognised as being of comparable significance for societies as the introduction of the Gutenberg printing press. As with the printing press, the significance of the internet arises not just from its facilitation of the dissemination and acquisition of information, but from the opportunities it creates for the format of viable businesses. The technology of the printing press lowered the unit cost of the codification and transmission of information, so that viable businesses could be formatted using printing presses. Similarly, the technology of the internet has lowered the unit cost of dissemination of information and opened opportunities for the format of viable companies.

The formats of internet companies depend mainly not on revenues from sale of information but on payments for the dissemination of information. Payments by advertisers are based on 'cost per contact', so that internet companies need to assemble the highest numbers of contacts to attract the greatest revenues. 'Contact' is also what internet companies such as Facebook and Tencent offer as a service. People use internet services to make contact with others, exchanging information on political, social and personal issues. The more contact, the better the service. Wide contact attracts people who make it wider. The best service to people in general is then also likely to be the most remunerative through provision of contacts for advertisers. Leading internet companies have grown to great size in a relatively short period through accumulation of contacts. Whilst the internet has provided opportunities for the emergence of very large companies, it has also provided opportunities for the dissemination of information by individuals on a scale that was inconceivable with older technology.

The importance of contacts in attracting advertising revenues for internet companies has substantially eroded the circulations of print media. Extensive information is provided free of charge over the internet. Some print media have established online editions, but experience difficulties in selling subscriptions to their online services. Some have adopted a format comparable to that of internet companies, distributing their product free of charge to reach the high circulations that attract advertising revenues.

Support-bargaining and money-bargaining are conducted on the basis of information. In political support-bargaining, open access to information is essential to the operation of a full support-bargaining system (Bite 11). Open circulation of information is then a primary communal interest. The normal agency for the advance of communal interests is government, but governments also have interests distinct from those of the community at large—specifically, the maintenance of support for their own continued governance. Consequently, while open circulation of information is recognised as a communal interest, the circulation of such information by governments is not recognised as a communal interest. It is recognised, in particular, that the provision of information solely by governments is contrary to communal interest. Thus, while it is unsatisfactory that something so prone to manipulation as information should be disseminated in accordance with a requirement to meet the corporate viability condition, it is the most effective way of meeting a communal interest in provision of information that is free from manipulation in accordance with the interests of government.

The United Kingdom nevertheless retains a government organisation for the dissemination of information as a matter of communal interest. The BBC operates 'at arm's length' from government, under a Royal Charter. Up to 2017, it was controlled by the BBC Trust; it is currently controlled by the BBC Board. It is financed by a license fee payable by all who receive television broadcasts. It is criticised by both right and left for bias in its coverage, and resented by commercial media organisations as unfair competition in the provision of information. It nevertheless has extensive support from people in general as a provider of dependable, wide-ranging and generally balanced information, and a provider of a variety of entertainment.

While media organisations must be primarily concerned with meeting the monetary viability condition, they invariably have some commitment, in some cases a very strong commitment, to the advance of particular interests. Some media are inclined to favour the left of the political spectrum; others the right. Buyers buy information in accordance with corresponding affiliations to left or right. Media propagating information with a left wing inclination find buyers on the left, and similarly media with a right wing inclination find right wing buyers. Media reflect the fundamental tension of support-bargaining between individual and group interests. Media organisations select and manipulate information for the advance of their political interests, subject to continuing fulfilment of their overriding interest in meeting the monetary viability condition.

This role of the media means that the conventional 'democratic' concept of media as mere reporters of what is going on misses their essential function (cf. Bite 11). They are an integral part of the process of government. They determine the information that reaches the general public and largely determine how it will be understood or interpreted. Their reports assemble support for their chosen interests, and that support is inevitably reflected in support for political parties. The media are reckoned to have had a highly influential, if not decisive, role in the outcome of the referendum in June 2016 on British membership of the European Union. 'Media studies' are often referred to with disdain, but the media have to be studied as an organ of government. Without an understanding of the media, there is no understanding of government.

The diversity of media is an essential safeguard for a support-bargaining society against the propagation of information in support of particular interests, and the suppression of other information. It is an aspect of the common 'multiple source' approach to the pursuit of dependable information (Bite 13). The existence of a state media organisation such as the BBC would not be acceptable in the absence of a variety of other sources of information. Nevertheless, the influence of the Murdoch media in Britain, particularly their support for Margaret Thatcher during her premiership in the 1980s, the rejection of Neil Kinnock in the 1992 General Election, and the support for Tony Blair in the 1998 Election, disturbed defenders of democratic principles.

Bite 28: The Pursuit of Truth

'The pursuit of truth' is almost universally recognised as amongst the most virtuous of undertakings. People pursuing 'the truth', whether natural scientists, social scientists, people of faith, or in other lines of enquiry, gather esteem and support in their societies for their efforts. The implication is that truth is important to a society.

There is an assumption also that truth is accessible (Bite 24). The traditional understanding of 'truth' in high theory relates to knowledge of something beyond the human mind, or beyond the information interface; an 'absolute' knowledge. 'Objective' truth is truth that is reckoned to be free of any influence of human cognitive processes. Ideas of truth are in Western societies inescapably tied up with ideas of divine revelation of truth. We know the truth about what is beyond our minds because deities have revealed it to us, working through the minds of selected humans. Truth is something sacrosanct and precious, to be approached with awe and wonder. It is vital to know such truth when the salvation of souls depends on it.

The theory of support-bargaining suggests that such knowledge is unobtainable; we are confined to the information and knowledge that can be contained in our minds. We are limited to whatever 'effective truths' or 'sufficient truths' we can discern in an information interface. The 'pursuit of truth' then becomes a matter of discerning what might constitute truth within such limitation.

Truth becomes a matter of consistency. In common theory (Bite 10), people discern truth when one piece of information is consistent with another. If someone says 'George has gone to town', and there is another piece of information, perhaps from someone in town, indicating that 'George is in town', then there is consistency, and the statements will be taken as true.

The understanding of truth in the religious context has perhaps been the basis of the common supposition that people are naturally inclined to seek the truth. 'Good people', at least, seek the truth, even if 'bad people' do not. Modern psychology has done little to alter this supposition. Behavioural theorists relate the quirks of human behaviour to what they take to be the appropriate reference for truth—mathematical accounts of what is rational. 'Bias' is deviation from the mathematically rational. It is assumed that humans aspire to act in accordance with truth. Behavioural theorists take their mathematical cue from neoclassical economic theory. Neoclassical theorists assert the objective truth of their theory on the basis of the mathematics in which it is codified. It is, however, a mainstay of support for the individualist interest that is so fundamental to the dynamic of support-bargaining. Human psychology has evolved to protect interests, not to pursue truth. We pursue truth when it is in our interests to do so; we pursue those aspects of truth which it is in our interests to know about. When it is in our interests to do so, we pursue non-truth interests at the expense of truth. People instinctively promulgate information calculated to advance their interests rather than promote truth (Bite 11).

They are faced then with the necessity of establishing that the information they promulgate for advance of their interests is accepted as truthful amongst those they are involved with; that it is consistent with other information. The frames of reference described in Bite 12 are the major means of meeting this necessity. Frames of reference cause people to observe and interpret in ways consistent with the frame of reference. So, if a frame of reference conducive to certain interests can be established in the information interface, people will observe and interpret in ways that are consistent with the interests of the creators of the frame. People will see that the information that advances the interests of the creators of the frame is consistent with the frame and consequently will be inclined to regard it as true. Religious frames of reference are exceptionally effective in this way. People observe and interpret in accordance with their religious frames of reference, and understand 'truth' as consistency with those frames of reference. The effect is particularly strong in the case of frames of reference which people have assimilated in childhood (Bite 24).

It was seen in Bite 13 that the most rigorous approach to consistency is apparent in the replicative testing by multiple testers of natural scientific method. The requirement for engagement of different testers suggests that the influence of preconceptions is eliminated, though concerns over shared frames of reference are not entirely eliminated. Natural scientists have come to recognise that what is accepted as proven is what is supported within scientific theory groups, and contingent on the emergence of no further information that might be inconsistent with the information used in establishing the proofs. In the social sciences, similar means are used to establish consistency, though limited by the nature of the phenomena at issue. They are limited also by the commitments of testers. Social scientific frames of reference are necessarily linked with political frames of reference. The conflict between individual and group is waged in both. Hence, the testing of social scientists for consistencies is likely to be influenced by preconceptions arising from political preferences.

'Multiple source' tests for consistency are used in specific circumstances across societies for the identification of 'truth' that can be accepted as adequately reliable, or as close as can practically be achieved, in the circumstances in which it is to be used. Common theory builds up understanding of 'truth' from observed consistencies like that relating to 'George in town' above. In common circumstances, such ready reckoning of truth is adequate, safeguarded as it is by certain qualifications regarding the reputation of speakers and other considerations.

Much of the information by which people determine their support for political factions is disseminated by media organisations which are primarily money-bargaining agencies (Bite 27). The interest in monetary viability tends to dominate the content that is provided. Media whose viability depends on large circulations at low prices tend to be undemanding with regard to what they will accept as sufficiently true to be published. A 'good story' is more important, because a 'good story' sells (cf. Bite 10). The 'quality' media are formatted for smaller circulations at higher prices. The requirements of their readers impose generally higher requirements for factual reliability.

In courts of law, statements are taken from multiple sources and assessed for their consistency. Judges and juries must take into account that the primary objective of an accused, and possibly also of some witnesses, is the advance of interests rather than the pursuit of truth. Conclusions have been found sufficient with regard to identification of the truth about crimes to sustain support for the system in society as a whole. Conclusions as to 'truth' are essential, so means are adopted that provide a version of truth that is acceptable in the circumstances. There are occasions when information comes to light subsequent to the conclusion of a trial which is inconsistent with the information provided in the course of the trial, and the truth of a verdict has to be reconsidered. Given the primacy of the pursuit of interest, such outcomes are almost inevitable.

The neoclassical economic model may be seen as a similarly localised approach to truth, based on the interests of a particular group. Economists responding to the question of the relationship between private and public interest created an illustrative mathematical model. The mathematical emphasis, and the limited concern for empirical evidence, made it easy to cultivate the model within academic confines. Notwithstanding many anomalies with observations of common theory, the neoclassical model was successfully established in academic institutions as the mainstream theory of economic behaviour, with all the accompanying incentives and rewards of institutional structures. The model provides a local understanding of truth based on the consistency of certain selected aspects of economic behaviour with a frame of reference. Social scientific frames of reference, however, as noted above, are almost inevitably associated with political frames of reference. The neoclassical model apparently reconciles individual interest with public interest. It advances the interests of one of the major factions of support-bargaining processes. So what is essentially a local interest in a conjecture of moral philosophy has been adopted amongst a much wider community in support of the individualist interest in society.

Consistency and hence truth can only be ascertained on the basis of available information. Any 'truth' is then always provisional. The pursuit of truth lies in building an information interface that is universally consistent, but the propensity of humans to disseminate information for advance of their interests, and to withhold information that is inimical to their interests, coupled with the inherent inaccessibility of information relevant to the full knowledge of particular circumstances, means that the information interface is inherently incomplete and distorted, so that it can never provide the comprehensive tests of consistency that establish truth. The jigsaw cannot be entirely fitted together to give the full picture when pieces have been hidden, or cannot be had, or are bent out of shape. The practical response is the establishment of a localised information interface that is adequate for the purpose in hand. It means also that 'truth' can never have the 'absolute' status that the word is commonly used to convey, and which would be justified if truth derived from divine revelation. 'Truth' has to be understood as something more pragmatic and approximate, resting on consistency and frames of reference.

'Consistency' is identified above as the critical test of 'truth'. The sense of 'consistency' arises, however, from the sense of symmetry. The sense of symmetry gives us our idea of how things fit together—how the jigsaw fits together. Inconsistency jars on our minds because inconsistencies do not fit together. Postmodern philosophers affirm that there is no logic by which it can be shown that the external world—a world beyond our minds—actually exists. They are undoubtedly right in that, but perhaps wrong in assuming that logical analysis is the appropriate method by which to assess the existence of an external world. Logic depends on consistencies, and is consequently also dependent on the broader sense of symmetry. Symmetry permeates all we know of the universe. Crucial developments in physics over the past two centuries have originated in the concept of symmetry. The symmetry of the universe seems incorporated in the particulate material of the universe, and hence would also be incorporated in humans, who are made of that same material. Our mental predilection for symmetry derives from our biological constitution, and thereby connects our minds with what we understand as an external world. Our sense of symmetry accords with our integration into the universal symmetry. We exist in the same way as the rest of the universe exists. The term 'information interface' implies that there is something beyond our minds to which information is an interface. Information forms an interface between our symmetries of mind and the symmetries of the rest of the universe. No form of words can bridge the gap between minds and any possible reality beyond, but the idea of symmetry takes probability to within a small part of a decimal point of certainty.

Notes from the Kitchen

Sources

Bite 23: Information and the Information Interface
Economics for an Information Age (EIA) is concerned with the use of information in support-bargaining and money-bargaining. Important references on general information, knowledge and psychology include: Goldman (2003), Kahneman (2012), Latour and Woolgar (1986), Searle (1996), and Berger and Luckman (1991/1966).

Bite 24: Information in a Bargaining System
The sections 'Paradigmatic perception and consumer choice' and '"Bounded rationality" and perceived fit' in Chapter 3 of *A Theory of Support and Money Bargaining* (TSMB) are concerned with the use of paradigms or frames of reference. The subject is introduced at pp. 10–11.

Frames of reference are considered in detail in Chapter 11 of *Support-Bargaining: The Mechanics of Democracy Revealed* (SBMDR), 'Frames and Echoes'. See sources under Bite 12.

On references, see Chapter 11, 'Anchors', in Kahneman (2012). On 'cognitive ease', see Chapter 5, 'Cognitive Ease' in Kahneman (2012).

On perceptual and testimonial information, see Steup (2014).

The sentence 'There is a long-standing tradition… true knowledge' is a quotation from Gregory (2004a).

The sub-section 'The distinctive impact of "electric" media' in Chapter 7 of EIA considers the presentation of testimonial information in perceptual form. The discussion centres on McLuhan (1964). See also Bite 25.

Bite 25: Codification and Transmission of Information
Chapter 8, 'Common Theory and Personification' in *Support-Bargaining, Economics and Society* (SBES), describes the use of personification. Sources include: Darwin (2004/1871), Beer (2008), Wilson (2000/1975), Wilson (2004/1978), Hamilton (1964), Kaye (1986), and Dawkins (2006/1976). The section 'Common theory and language' in the same chapter is concerned with language, drawing principally on Pinker (1994).

On the first writing in Britain, see Howgego (2016).

Chapter 9, 'Information and the Evolution of Communications', of *The Evolution of Economies* (TEOE) deals with aspects of codification and transmission. See in particular sub-sections on 'Codification: the printing press', 'Transmission of information' and 'Viability of transmitting companies'. This chapter is also concerned with an information infrastructure. Chapter 4, 'Economics and the Information Interface', of EIA (p. 133) covers briefly the technology of printing and its impact.

Chapter 7, 'Media Theory and the Information Interface', of EIA covers in more detail the changes brought about by innovations in print technology and other information technologies. Sources include Poe (2011) and Patterson (1990). Marshall McLuhan's (1964) ideas are considered in detail in this chapter.

The section 'Akerlof and asymmetric information' in Chapter 4, 'Economics and the Information Interface', of EIA deals with George Akerlof's (1970) account of quality. The same chapter deals with other aspects of information and the formulation of the neoclassical economic model. See under Bites 13 and 18 for sources. Stigler's comment on quality is in Stigler (1961, p. 61). See also TSMB, pp. 50–1; Chapter 1 of EIA, pp. 23–4.

On the priority accorded to mathematical codification, see Hodgson (1988, pp. 73–4), Backhouse (1993, p. 196; 1994, pp. 221–2), see also Spread (2011); TEOE, pp. ix, 49–55, 317.

Briggs and Burke (2009) is indicative of the limitations of information theory.

Bite 26: Information in Money-Bargaining

The sections 'Neoclassical economic theory and information' and 'Knowledge and institutions' in Chapter 1 of EIA discuss work on the economics of information. Sources include: Akerlof and Shiller (2015), Stigler (1961), Fransman (1994), Alchian and Demsetz (1972) (see Fransman (1994, pp. 718–19)), Jensen and Meckling (1976), Simon (1957, 1997/1947, 1983), Williamson (1987), March and Simon (1993/1958), Nelson and Winter (1982), Molho (2001), Spence (1973), Hayek (1952), Akerlof (1970), Richardson (1990/1960, 1998), Foss and Loasby (2013), Phlips (1988), Casson (2000), Lamberton (1971, 1996), Dow (2017), Loasby (1999), Lancaster (1981), and Earl (2002). See also Spread (2011, 2015a, 2016b).

The sections 'Akerlof and asymmetric information' and 'Stiglitz and the neoclassical frame of reference' in Chapter 4 of EIA deal with Akerlof's and Stiglitz's accounts of 'asymmetric information' and Stiglitz's views on paradigm change. Sources include: Akerlof (1970), Stiglitz (1985, 2002). Chapter 9 of TEOE has sections on 'Information and neoclassical economics' and 'Beyond asymmetries'.

The sections 'Money-bargaining and the information interface' and 'Communal interest and government' in Chapter 4 of EIA cover the role of information in money-bargaining. The sections draw on: Richardson (1990/1960), Searle (1996), and Heilbroner (2000).

Some Chicago School economists treat information as a commodity (Stiglitz 2002, p. 462). Cortada (2016), treats information as a commodity, exchanged by educated people.

Bite 27: Role of Media in Governance

Chapter 7, 'Media Theory and the Information Interface', of EIA deals with theories concerning the role of media, drawing particularly on: Innis (1950), Poe (2011), Hugo (2015/1831), and McLuhan (1964). Other sources are: Finkelstein (1968), Briggs and Burke (2009), Goldman (2003), and Patterson (1990).

Chapter 8, 'Media, Governance and the Information Interface', is concerned with the process of government and the formation of a political information interface. The chapter draws particularly on: Davies (2015) and Price (2010). The role of the Murdoch group in British politics features in Leveson (2012). The opening section of Chapter 8 of EIA covers Goldman's (2003, pp. 340–2) account of the role of the press in a democracy.

The sub-section 'Codification: the printing press' in Chapter 9 of TEOE covers the business opportunities arising from the printing press.

On the influence of the press on the outcome of the Referendum in 2016 on Britain's membership of the European Union, see Ponsford (2016a, b).

Bite 28: The Pursuit of Truth

Chapter 1, 'Information and Interests', Chapter 2, 'Support-Bargaining and the Information Interface' and Chapter 6, 'The Information Interface and Reality', of EIA discuss truth, facts, frames of reference, interests and the existence of an external world. Important sources include: Goldman (2003), Searle (1996), Berger and Luckman (1991), and Latour and Woolgar (1986).

Chapter 5, 'Economics and Behavioural Economics', is concerned with the influence of behavioural theory on neoclassical economic theory. Sources include: Bruni and Sugden (2007), Simon (1956, 1983, 1997/1947), Earl (1988, 1995), Kahnman and Tversky (1979), Kahneman (2003, 2012), Kahneman and Frederick (2002), Gigerenzer et al. (1989), Gigerenzer (1991), and World Bank (2015).

On symmetry, see Chapter 10, 'Social Symmetries', in SBES. Sources include: Stewart and Golubitsky (1992), Sautoy (2008), Feynman et al. (1964), and Pinker (1994).

The section 'The status of theories' in Chapter 7 of SBES considers the pursuit of truth and the pursuit of interest. Sources include: Crook (1994), Hofstadter (1983/1944), Bannister (1979), and Kaye (1986), see also Dow (2017).

References

Akerlof, George A., 1970, 'The Market for "Lemons": Quality Uncertainty and the Market Mechanism', *Quarterly Journal of Economics*, Vol. 84, No. 3, pp. 488–500.

Akerlof, George A., and Shiller, Robert, 2015, *Phishing for Phools*, Princeton University Press.

Alchian, A., and Demsetz, H., 1972, 'Production, Information Costs, and Economic Organization', *The American Economic Review*, Vol. 62, pp. 777–95.

Backhouse, Roger E., 1993, *Economists and the Economy: The Evolution of Economic Ideas*, Transaction.

Backhouse, Roger E., 1994, *Economists and the Economy: The Evolution of Economic Ideas*, Second Edition, Transaction.

Bannister, Robert, 1979, *Social Darwinism: Science and Myth in Anglo-American Social Thought*, Philadelphia: Temple University Press.

Beer, Gillian, 2008, Introduction to Darwin, 2008/1859.

Berger, Peter, and Luckman, Thomas, 1991/1966, *The Social Construction of Reality*, Penguin. First Published 1966.

Briggs, Asa, and Burke, Peter, 2009, *A Social History of the Media: From Gutenberg to the Internet*, Third Edition, Polity Press.

Bruni, Luigino, and Sugden, Robert, 2007, 'The Road Not Taken: How Psychology Was Removed from Economics, and How It Might Be Brought Back', *The Economic Journal*, Vol. 117, No. 516, pp. 146–73.

Casson, Mark, 2000, 'An Entrepreneurial Theory of the Firm', in Foss and Mahuke, pp. 116–45.

Cortada, James W., 2016, *All the Facts: A History of Information in the United States Since 1870*, Oxford University Press.

Crook, Paul, 1994, *Darwinism, War and History*, Cambridge University Press.

Darwin, Charles, 2004/1871, *The Descent of Man, and Selection in Relation to Sex*, Penguin. First Published 1871.

Davies, Nick, 2015, *Hack Attack: How the Truth Caught Up with Rupert Murdoch*, Vintage Books.

Dawkins, Richard, 2006/1976, *The Selfish Gene*, Oxford University Press. First Published 1976.

Dow, Sheila, 2017, 'How Far Are Economists Purveyors of Fake News?', Annual Conference of the Institute for New Economic Thinking, October. https://www.ineteconomics.org/research/research-papers/how-far-are-economists-purveyors-of-fake-news. Accessed 12 January 2018.

du Sautoy, Marcus, 2008, *Symmetry: A Journey into the Patterns of Nature*, HarperCollins. First Published in Great Britain 2008 as *Finding Moonshine*, Fourth Estate.

Earl, Peter E. (Ed.), 1988, *Behavioural Economics*, Edward Elgar.

Earl, Peter E., 1995, *Microeconomics for Business and Marketing*, Edward Elgar.

Earl, Peter E. (Ed.), 2002, *Information, Opportunism and Economic Coordination*, Edward Elgar.

Feynman, Richard P., Leighton, Robert B., and Sands, Matthew, 1964, *The Feynman Lectures on Physics, Volume 1*, Addison-Wesley.

Finkelstein, Sidney, 1968, *Sense and Nonsense of McLuhan*, International Publishers.

Foss, Nicolai, and Loasby, Brian (Eds.), 2013, *Introduction to Economic Organization, Capabilities and Coordination: Essays in Honour of G. B. Richardson*, Electronic Resource, Bodleian Library and Oxford: Routledge.

Foss, Nicolai, and Mahuke, Volker (Eds.), 2000, *Competence, Governance and Entrepreneurship*, Oxford University Press.

Fransman, M. 1994. 'Information, Knowledge, Vision and Theories of the Firm', *Industrial and Corporate Change*, Vol. 3, No. 3, pp. 713–57.

Galatin, Malcolm, and Leiter, Robert D., 1981, *The Economics of Information*, Martinus Nijhoff Publishing.

Gigerenzer, Gerd, 1991, 'How to Make Cognitive Illusions Disappear: Beyond "Heuristics and Biases"', in Stroebe and Hewstone, 1991.

Goldman, Alvin I., 2003, *Knowledge in a Social World*, Clarendon Press.

Gregory, Richard L., 2004a, 'Perception', in Gregory, 2004b.

Gregory, Richard L. (Ed.), 2004b, *The Oxford Companion to the Mind*, Oxford University Press.

Gigerenzer, G., Swijtink, Z., Porter, T., Daston, L., Beatty, J., and Kruger, L., 1989, *The Empire of Chance: How Probability Changed Science and Everyday Life*, Cambridge University Press.
Hamilton, W. D., 1964, 'The Genetic Evolution of Social Behavior, I and II', *Journal of Theoretical Biology*, Vol. 7, pp. 1–51.
Hayek, Friedrich A., 1952, *The Sensory Order, An Enquiry into the Foundations of Theoretical Psychology*, University of Chicago.
Heilbroner, Robert, 2000, *The Worldly Philosophers: The Lives, Theories and Ideas of the Great Economic Thinkers*, Penguin. First Published 1953.
Hodgson, G. M., 1988, *Economics and Institutions*, Polity Press.
Hofstadter, Richard, 1983/1944, *Social Darwinism in American Thought*, Beacon Press. First Published 1944.
Howgego, Joshua, 2016, 'Britain's Oldest Writing Found Buried Near London Tube Station', *New Scientist*, June 1. https://www.newscientist.com/article/2091213-britains-oldest-writing-found-buried-near-london-tube-station/. Accessed 30 April 2018.
Hugo, Victor, 2015/1831, *The Hunchback of Notre Dame*, Waxkeep Publishing, Kindle Edition. First Published 1831.
Innis, Harold, 1950, *Empire and Communications*, Oxford University Press.
Jensen, M., and Meckling, W., 1976. 'Theory of the Firm: Managerial Behaviour, Agency Costs, and Ownership Structure', *The Journal of Financial Economics*, Vol. 3, pp. 305–60.
Kahneman, Daniel, and Frederick, Shane, 2002, 'Representativeness Revisited: Attribution Substitution in Intuitive Judgement', in Gilovich, Griffin and Kahneman, 2002.
Kahneman, Daniel, 2003, 'Maps of Bounded Rationality: Psychology for Behavioural Economics', *American Economic Review*, Vol. 93, No. 5, pp. 1449–75.
Kahneman, Daniel, 2012, *Thinking, Fast and Slow*, Penguin.
Kahneman, Daniel, and Tversky, Amos, 1979, 'Prospect Theory: An Analysis of Decision Under Risk', *Econometrica*, Vol. 47, No. 2, pp. 263–91.
Kaye, Howard, 1986, *The Social Meaning of Modern Biology*, Yale University Press.
Lamberton, D. M. (Ed.), 1971, *Economics of Information and Knowledge*, Penguin.
Lamberton, D. M. (Ed.), 1996, *The Economics of Communication and Information*, Edward Elgar.
Lancaster, Kelvin J., 1981, 'Information and Product Differentiation', in Galatin and Leiter, 1981.
Latour, Bruno, and Woolgar, Steve, 1986, *Laboratory Life: The Construction of Scientific Facts*, University Press.

Leveson, Lord Justice Brian, 2012, *An Inquiry into the Culture, Practices and Ethics of the Press,* Volumes 1–4, Department of Culture, Media and Sport, Leveson Inquiry.

Loasby, Brian, 1999, *Knowledge, Institutions and Evolution in Economics*, Routledge.

March, James, and Simon, Herbert, 1993/1958, *Organisations*, Blackwell Business. First Published 1958.

McLuhan, Marshall, 1964, *Understanding Media: The Extensions of Man*, Routledge.

Molho, Ian, 2001, *The Economics of Information: Lying and Cheating in Markets and Organisations*, Blackwell.

Nelson, Richard R., and Winter, Stanley G., 1982, *An Evolutionary Theory of Economic Change*, Belknap Press.

Patterson, Graeme H., 1990, *History and Communications: Harold Innis, Marshall McLuhan, the Interpretation of History*, University of Toronto.

Phlips, Louis, 1988, *The Economics of Imperfect Information*, Cambridge University Press.

Pinker, Steven, 1994, *The Language Instinct*, Penguin.

Poe, Marshall T., 2011, *A History of Communications: Media and Society from the Evolution of Speech to the Internet*, Cambridge University Press.

Ponsford, Dominic, 2016a, 'Strong UK National Press Bias in Favour of Leave Revealed by Press Gazette's Brexitometer Front-Page Tracker', *Press Gazette*, 16 June 2016.

Ponsford, Dominic, 2016b, 'EU Referendum: Why It May Have Been the Telegraph, Sun, Express and Mail "Wot Won It" for Leave', *Press Gazette*, 24 June 2016.

Price, Lance, 2010, *Where Power Lies: Prime Ministers v The Media*, Simon and Schuster.

Richardson, George B., 1990/1960, *Information and Investment: A Study in the Working of the Competitive Economy*, Second Edition, Oxford University Press. First Published 1960.

Richardson, George B., 1998, *The Economics of Imperfect Knowledge: Collected Papers of G. B. Richardson*, Edward Elgar.

Searle, John, 1996, *The Construction of Social Reality*, Penguin.

Simon, Herbert A., 1956, 'Rational Choice and the Structure of the Environment', *Psychological Review*, Vol. 63, No. 2, pp. 129–38.

Simon, Herbert A., 1957, *Models of Man: Social and Rational: Mathematical Essays on Rational Human Behavior in a Social Setting*, Wiley.

Simon, Herbert A., 1983, *Reason in Human Affairs*, Stanford University Press.

Simon, Herbert A., 1997/1947, *Administrative Behaviour: A Study of Decision-Making Processes in Administrative Organizations*, Free Press. First Published 1947.

Spence, Michael, 1973, 'Job Market Signalling', *Quarterly Journal of Economics*, Vol. 87, No. 3, pp. 355–74.

Spread, Patrick, 1984, *A Theory of Support and Money Bargaining (TSMB)*, Macmillan.

Spread, Patrick, 2008, *Support-Bargaining: The Mechanics of Democracy Revealed (SBMDR)*, Book Guild.

Spread, Patrick, 2011, 'Situation as Determinant of Selection and Valuation', *Cambridge Journal of Economics*, Vol. 35, No. 2. Reprinted in Spread, 2015b.

Spread, Patrick, 2013, *Support-Bargaining, Economics and Society: A Social Species (SBES)*, Routledge.

Spread, Patrick, 2015a, 'Asymmetric Information, Critical Information and the Information Interface', *Real-World Economics Review*, No. 70, pp. 121–40. Reprinted in Spread, 2015b.

Spread, Patrick, 2015b, *Aspects of Support-Bargaining and Money-Bargaining (ASBMB)*, E-Book, World Economics Association.

Spread, Patrick, 2016a, *The Evolution of Economies: Money-Bargaining, Economic Change and Industrial Revolution (TEOE)*, Routledge.

Spread, Patrick, 2016b, 'Companies and Markets: Economic Theories of the Firm and a Concept of Companies as Bargaining Agencies', *Cambridge Journal of Economics*, Vol. 40, No. 3, pp. 727–53, Online at Doi. 2015. https://doi.org/10.1093/cje/bev029. Reprinted in Spread, 2015b.

Spread, Patrick, 2019, *Economics for an Information Age: Money-Bargaining, Support-Bargaining and the Information Interface (EIA)*, Routledge.

Steup, Mathias, 2014, 'Epistemology', in Zalta, 2014.

Stewart, Ian, and Golubitsky, Martin, 1992, *Fearful Symmetry: Is God a Geometer?* Penguin.

Stigler, G. J., 1961, 'The Economics of Information', *Journal of Political Economy*, Vol. 69, pp. 213–25. Reprinted in Lamberton, 1971.

Stiglitz, Joseph E., 1985, 'Information and Economic Analysis: A Perspective', *The Economic Journal*, Vol. 95, Supplement, pp. 21–41.

Stiglitz, Joseph E., 2002, 'Information and the Change in the Paradigm in Economics', *American Economic Review*, Vol. 92, No. 3, pp. 460–501.

Williamson, O. E., 1987, *The Economic Institutions of Capitalism*, Free Press.

Wilson, Edward O., 2000/1975, *Sociobiology: The New Synthesis*, Belknap Press. First Published 1975.

Wilson, Edward O., 2004/1978, *On Human Nature*, Harvard University Press. First Published 1978.

World Bank, 2015, *World Development Report 2015: Mind, Society and Behaviour*, World Bank.

Zalta, Edward N. (Ed.), 2014, *The Stanford Encyclopedia of Philosophy*, Spring Edition, 4, Sources of Knowledge and Justification. http://plato.stanford.edu/archives/spr2014/entries/epistemology/. Accessed 28 December 2017.

The Main Course

Books on Support-Bargaining and Money-Bargaining

The idea of support-bargaining was first set out in *A Theory of Support and Money Bargaining* (TSMB), published in 1984 by Macmillan. This was written on a PhD programme at the London Business School. It provides a basic account of the theory at a formative stage. Engagement in the PhD programme made it possible to consult a wide range of literature related in some way to the proposed theory of support-bargaining and money-bargaining, so the book covers a wide range of academic literature. It was possible also to see if what was then a one-man embryonic theory would be knocked down or made redundant by closer attention to what others had written.

The next publication on the subject came some years later. *Getting It Right: Economics and the Security of Support* (GIR) was published in 2004 by the Book Guild. This was conceived as a more theoretically mature and accessible book on support-bargaining and money-bargaining. It was written outside the academic environment and after considerable experience 'road-testing' the theory in the context of socio-economic development in various countries. It contrasts the neoclassical economic model with the theory of money-bargaining (Bite 18). It describes situation-related selection (Bite 3) and the role of organisations (Bite 5). It also associates rigid groups with violence (Bite 6).

P. Spread, *A Starter on Support-Bargaining and Money-Bargaining in Twenty-Eight Digestible Bites*,
https://doi.org/10.1007/978-3-030-05231-7

Support-Bargaining: The Mechanics of Democracy Revealed (SBMDR) was published by the Book Guild in 2008. This developed the theory of support-bargaining and money-bargaining. It provides a detailed account of informal and formal group support-bargaining (Bites 1–9). The idea of 'intellectual support-bargaining' is prominent (Bites 10–13). The formation of theory assembles support and is consequently part of the political process. The 'mechanics' of democracy includes the process of theory formation. Theories such as neoclassical economics and socialist theory fulfil political purposes as well as seeking to explain the functioning of societies (Bite 12). Situation is identified as the basis of consumer selection (Bite 15). The idea of companies as bargaining agencies is developed in terms of set-related and cost-related efficiencies (Bite 16). This book constitutes the basic statement of the theory of support-bargaining and money-bargaining.

The role of support-bargaining in human survival was investigated in *Support-Bargaining, Economics and Society: A Social Species* (SBES), published by Routledge in 2013. The opening chapter explains how support-bargaining is necessary to the explanation of natural selection (Bite 1). Chapter 8 is on 'Common theory and personification' (Bite 10). The same chapter covers the role of language in support-bargaining (Bite 1). Chapter 3, on 'Power and hierarchy', is concerned with the exercise of 'power' through the assembly of support, the institution of hierarchy and the use of money (Bites 1–5, 22). Chapter 9 covers the origins of money and the social implications of money-bargaining (Bite 14). Chapter 10 is concerned with 'Social symmetries', including 'Symmetry and common theory' (Bites 3, 28).

The Evolution of Economies: Money-Bargaining, Economic Change and Industrial Revolution (TEOE), published by Routledge in 2016, is principally concerned to establish the dynamic of economic evolution in terms of movement from situation to situation (Bite 3). The industrial revolution is explained by reference to the function of companies as bargaining agencies (Bite 16). Company formats central to the industrial revolution were identified in cotton, iron and railways. That period saw the evolution of the British economy from a situation in which ordinary people were dependent on landowners for their livelihoods to dependence on companies for employment and incomes. The book seeks to explain also how neoclassical economic theory came to dominate academic theory (Bite 18). It describes also the links between support-bargaining and money-bargaining (Bite 22).

Aspects of Support-Bargaining and Money-Bargaining (ASBMB) was published by the World Economics Association (WEA) as an E-Book in 2015 (www.worldeconomicsassociation.org/books/). It comprises six previously published articles and two previously unpublished. The reprints include those on situation-related selection (Bite 3) and the role of companies (Bite 16).

Economics for an Information Age: Money-Bargaining, Support-Bargaining and the Information Interface (EIA) was published by Routledge in 2019. It is concerned with the creation and role of an information interface in support-bargaining and money-bargaining, including the use of frames of reference and the manipulation of information (Bites 12, 23–28). A section on 'Neoclassical economic theory and information' in Chapter 1 appraises the efforts of neoclassical economists to reconcile information issues with the neoclassical model. Chapter 4 describes the role of information in money-bargaining (Bite 26), including a section on 'Communal interest and government' (Bite 20). Chapter 5, 'Economics and behavioural economics', assesses the impact of behavioural economics on mainstream economic theory (Bite 28). Chapter 6, 'The Information Interface and Reality', describes an 'informationist ontology' that definitively denies human access to secure knowledge of what is beyond our minds (Bite 28). Chapters 7 and 8 cover the essential role of media organisations in disseminating the information essential to the functioning of a support-bargaining society (Bite 27).

Index

P. Spread, *A Starter on Support-Bargaining and Money-Bargaining in Twenty-Eight Digestible Bites*,
https://doi.org/10.1007/978-3-030-05231-7

The manufacturer's authorised representative in the EU is Springer Nature Customer Service Centre GmbH, Europaplatz 3, 69115 Heidelberg, Germany. If you have any concerns regarding our products, please contact ProductSafety@springernature.com

Printed and bound by CPI Group (UK) Ltd, Croydon, CR0 4YY
25/09/2026
02222890-0019